THE STING OF THE LUFTWAFFE

THE STING OF THE LUFTWAFFE

Schnellkampfgeschwader 210 and Zerstörergeschwader 1
"Wespengeschwader" in World War II

John Vasco

Schiffer Military History
Atglen, PA

Acknowledgements

Without reference to the volume of their respective contributions, I would like to thank the following former members of Schnellkampfgeschwader 210 and Zerstörergeschwader 1 for their assistance: Otto Atz; Wilhelm Dibowski; Willi Falkenroth; Edwin Hess; Leo Kabacinski; Herbert Klinke; Franz Knäuper; Heinz Ludwig; Helmut Lußky; Heinz Lüttman; Kurt Meier; Wolfgang Meyer-Erlach; Heinz Natzinger; Rolf Rohrschneider; Wolfgang Schenck; Gerhard Schlee; Karl-Fritz Schröder; Willy Schwarz; Manfred Theves; Rudolf Thomas; Karl-Hans Trüdinger; Wolfgang Zander.

Relatives of former members who were killed or missing in action, or who had died since the end of the war, also provided assistance with information and photographs, and I thank Maria Scherberich (sister of Paul Karwatka); Wilfried Brandes (brother of Heinz Brandes); Uwe Steenbock (son of Kurt Steenbock); Lina Herkle-Rapp (widow of Paul Rapp); Hedwig Schmidt, (sister of Georg Reuther); Frieda Bielfeld, (sister of Hans Stoltenberg); Heinrich Martin, (brother of Rudolf Martin); Isolda Tratt, (widow of Eduard Tratt); Gertrude Günther, (niece of Ludwig Kastner); Elfriede Häuser, (sister of Werner Hess); Eugen Hummel, (nephew of Franz Hummel); Elsbeth Knackendöffel, (sister of Herbert Oerzmann); Horst Mayer, (brother of Heinz Mayer); Ulrich Sollfrank, (nephew of Dominikus Kneidl; Anni Jans (sister of Josef Dors); Helene Steinmann, (sister of Heinrich Bartling); Annemarie Mertens (widow of Otto Lusser); Karin Kessler (sister of Kurt Berns); Heinz Körner (brother of Gerhard Körner); Johann Licht, (brother of Hubert Licht).

The following researchers also provided valuable help: Peter Cornwell; Jean-Louis Roba; Eric Mombeek; Peter Petrick; Jan Bobek Jr. and Ron MacKay.

I would also like to thank the staff of the Deutsche Dienststelle (WAst) in Berlin and the Imperial War Museum, London for their assistance in the compilation of the loss/damage tables.

Dust jacket artwork by Steve Ferguson, Colorado Springs, CO.

WINTER WESPEN

The cover depicts a flight of ZG 1 Bf 110F-2 *Wespen* strafing Russian Airacobras on their snowbound airfield in the winter of 1942-43. Such missions marked the end of the big Messerschmitt fighters heyday on the eastern front as more tactical units would switch to the swifter Fw 190 fighter-bomber during the "great retreats" of 1943 and 1944.

Dedication

This book is dedicated to Karl-Fritz Schröder (23/5/1920-18/5/1999), Bordfunker of 3. Staffel, Schnellkampfgeschwader 210 and Zerstörergeschwader 1. In this life we have many acquaintances and very few friends. Karl was a dear friend.

Book design by Robert Biondi.

Library of Congress Catalog Number: 00-110387.

Printed in China.
ISBN: 0-7643-1305-3

We are always looking for people to write books on new and related subjects. If you have an idea for a book, please contact us at the address below.

Published by Schiffer Publishing Ltd.
4880 Lower Valley Road
Atglen, PA 19310
Phone: (610) 593-1777
FAX: (610) 593-2002
E-mail: Schifferbk@aol.com.
Visit our web site at: www.schifferbooks.com
Please write for a free catalog.
This book may be purchased from the publisher.
Please include $3.95 postage.
Try your bookstore first.

In Europe, Schiffer books are distributed by:
Bushwood Books
6 Marksbury Ave.
Kew Gardens
Surrey TW9 4JF
England
Phone: 44 (0)208 392-8585
FAX: 44 (0)208 392-9876
E-mail: Bushwd@aol.com.
Free postage in the UK. Europe: air mail at cost.
Try your bookstore first.

Preface

This work arose out of my research for my book on Erprobungsgruppe 210. During the course of that research in Germany, at the many 'Wespentreffen' which I attended, I met many former members of Schnellkampfgeschwader 210 and Zerstörergeschwader 1, who made me most welcome, and were curious why this Englishman had such an interest in matters Luftwaffe. I, in turn, realised that the units in which they flew and fought had received comparatively little recognition across the whole canvas of Luftwaffe operations in World War II. For example, pick up any book on Stalingrad and most will have little mention of air operations. The scant few which deign to mention Luftwaffe activity concentrate almost exclusively on the attempt to supply the German forces trapped in the Russian encirclement, and occasionally fighter escort missions are mentioned. You will find nothing of the attempts of the crews of Zerstörergeschwader 1 in the fighter-bomber role to open a gap in the encirclement so that German troops could regain their own lines. Many times I sat before old men who, with the mist of youth before their eyes, were back in the cockpit of their aircraft, recounting in a matter-of-fact manner the sheer terror of flying mission after mission in an attempt to force an opening; of knowing they would be flying low-level attacks into the teeth of accurate, concentrated flak defences; of limping back to base with a damaged or knocked-out engine, or damaged flying controls and not knowing at any moment whether their 'mill' would fall out of the sky taking them to their deaths, and of them seeing their youthful comrades in aircraft alongside them blown to pieces, or spiralling down out of control to a certain fate. Their experience was the experience of all who flew in war.

Aircrew and aircraft of Schnellkampfgeschwader 210 and Zerstörergeschwader 1 flew missions against England, took part in the heady, early days of the Russian campaign when German forces swept all before them, flew in the baking heat of the Mediterranean campaign when the odds were inexorably shifting against them, in missions in the Bay of Biscay and out into the Atlantic, and in Reich defence duties at a time when the American day fighters had honed to perfection the art of forward interception of intercepting Luftwaffe fighters. In the final days of the unit, losses were being suffered in the air battle following the Allied landings in Normandy, and in the desperate attempt to stem the incursions of allied bombers over Hungarian airspace. Their theatres of operations exceeded those of other Luftwaffe units.

As young men they flew and fought because of the call to arms of their native country. In the post-war years it is hard to understand the perceived guilt carried by some of them once the full horrors of the Third Reich regime for which they fought were laid bare before them. This was brought home to me in a totally unexpected way on the last morning of one of the 'Wespentreffen' which I attended. From amidst the hubbub of 'Wespen' guests departing from the reception area of the Hotel Selau in Neunkirchen-am-Brand one member approached me. I had not met him before, and we had not had occasion to talk during the Treffen, but he had obviously found out who I was, and why I was there. He offered me his hand, and in faltering English said: "Mr. Vasco, ... perhaps now I know we are friends again". He then took his leave of me, picked up his luggage and headed into the car park. For one man, my attendance may have changed, to some small degree, the perceptions which he must have carried for many years, of how people of other nations, and different generations, saw him and his generation.

In putting together this record of the Wespengeschwader, I could not possibly do justice to writing a full account of the period 1941-1944, since the lack of complete records militates against such an approach. I can only therefore offer this photographic record, with supporting text and appendices, to give the reader a snapshot of the men and machines of one unit which formed part of the Luftwaffe. This work seeks neither to glorify what took place, nor to take sides on any issue. It is simply the photographic record of young men. This is their silent story, not mine.

John Vasco
Norwich, England
June 2000

Schnellkampfgeschwader 210 and Zerstörergeschwader 1 "Wespengeschwader" in World War II

Origins

On 24 April 1941 Schnellkampfgeschwader 210 (Fast Bomber Wing 210) [SKG 210] came into existence, with the German offensive against the Soviet Union only weeks away. The Geschwader was formed principally from two existing Gruppen: the new I. Gruppe incorporated Erprobungsgruppe 210 (Erpr. Gr. 210); II. Gruppe took in the personnel from III. Gruppe, Zerstörergeschwader 76 (III./ZG 76). Although the unit was titled as a 'Geschwader', normally three Gruppen strength, it only consisted of two Gruppen. A III. Gruppe would only come into existence once it was redesignated in January 1942.

Erprobungsgruppe 210 had been formed in July 1940 and had seen fierce, almost continual, combat during the Battle of Britain in that year. The award of the 'Ritterkreuz' (Knights Cross) to four members of that single Gruppe (three posthumously) bore stark testimony to the cauldron of battle which the unit had gone through, and to the fighting qualities of the recipients and the men they led.

III. Gruppe, Zerstörergeschwader 76 was also a veteran unit of the Battle of Britain, having been redesignated from II. Gruppe, Zerstörergeschwader 1 prior to the commencement of the Battle and taken its share of Zerstörer losses in that campaign.

That part of the unit name '210' alluded to the fact that back in July 1940 expectations were high that the Messerschmitt 210 would be brought into service via Erprobungsgruppe 210, and that belief persisted into 1941 with the continuation of the reference in the new unit's name.

Major Walter Storp was posted-in as Geschwaderkommodore, with Hauptmann Karl-Heinz Stricker commanding I. Gruppe and Hauptmann Rolf Kaldrack leading II. Gruppe. Storp had previously served with Kampfgeschwader 30, and whereas he did not receive the Knights Cross, but survived the war, his Gruppenkommandeure would receive the Knights Cross and the Knights Cross with Oakleaves respectively, but would both be killed in action. Karl-Heinz Stricker had formerly served with Kampfgeschwader 26, and upon hearing of his appointment to lead the former 'Erprobungsgruppe' he went to Rechlin to find out all about this 'E-Gruppe'. Asking Haupt.-Ing. Rauchensteiner at Rechlin, he was told: "... E-Gruppe? – that is Schenck, nobody else, Schenck IS the E-Gruppe!..." Wolfgang Schenck's involvement in the 'E-Gruppe' started when he joined Erprobungsgruppe 210 on 4 September 1940 after recovering from injuries received in combat during the Battle of France. Before the end of the year he was Staffelkapitän of 1st Staffel, and developed a deep interest in advancing the capabilities of 'Zerstörer' aircraft. By the time Karl-Heinz Stricker came onto the 'Zerstörer' scene, Schenck's interest and involvement was widely known.

Into Action

In the early months of 1941 Erprobungsgruppe 210 carried out missions against targets on the south-east coast of England, and against shipping. Upon redesignation to I. Gruppe, Schnellkampfgeschwader 210 they continued with those missions, and continued to suffer occasional losses. II. Gruppe meanwhile were working up on their new role as fighter-bombers.

The opening of the campaign against the Soviet Union on 22 June 1941 saw Schnellkampfgeschwader 210 pitched into action, both Gruppen operating from the outset under II. Fliegerkorps. Missions continued apace following the rapid advance of the German ground forces in the first months of the conflict; no respite was taken until I. Gruppe was taken out of the line in October 1941 to return to Germany and begin conversion to the ill-fated Messerschmitt 210 A.

The 'meat-grinder' that was the Russian front was to take a continual toll of Luftwaffe aircrew, and Schnellkampfgeschwader 210 was no exception; the hazardous low-level attacks which they conducted made them prime targets for the Russian anti-aircraft batteries. In 1941, while claiming continuing success against allotted ground targets as well as aerial victories, the unit lost one Gruppenkommandeur, Hauptmann Karl-Heinz Stricker of I. Gruppe on 13th September 1941, and four Staffelkapitäne.

Erprobungsstaffel 210/Messerschmitt 210

Early in 1941 the 'Erprobungsstaffel 210' was formed at Rechlin, ostensibly to work the Messerschmitt 210 up to operational status. Major Walter Storp was the driving force behind the setting-up of the Staffel. The first Commanding Officer of the Staffel, Oberleutnant Weyert, crashed to his death in early April 1941. His place was taken by Hauptmann Heinz Nacke on 12 April 1941, who led the testing until succeeded by Oberleutnant Heinz Forgatsch, Staffelkapitän of 3. Staffel, Schnellkampfgeschwader 210, on 14 August 1941. Forgatsch had flown with 2. Staffel, Erprobungsgruppe 210 during the Battle of Britain, and was appointed Staffelkapitän of 3. Staffel when it was re-formed with Bf 110s towards the end of 1940. On 23 September 1941 Forgatsch crashed to his death with his Bordfunker, Feldwebel Kurt Hoffmann, at Ankershagen, north-west of Rechlin, in a Me 210 A-1 during a test flight. Wolfgang Schenck succeeded Forgatsch as Commanding Officer of Erprobungsstaffel 210 on 24 September 1941, and while 'dog-fighting' with Oberleutnant Walter Maurer in Me 210s, Maurer's machine went into a 'flat spin', but he lived to tell the tale. It was established that this was the cause of the many crashes which had happened, and that the problem occurred within a small speed range either side of 450 Kilometres per hour. Maurer had a chequered career in the Luftwaffe. He was with 3. Staffel, Zerstörergeschwader 2 at the outbreak of war, flying a Bf 109 and claiming his first combat victory. Operating out of Darmstadt at the opening of the Western Campaign in May 1940, he was shot down in a Bf 110 on 11 May and became a prisoner of the French. Released from French captivity, he was eventually posted to ZG 76 and joined the Staff Flight of II. Gruppe, Schnellkampfgeschwader 210 upon its formation in April 1941. After service on the Russian front, he moved in October 1941 to Rechlin to join the Messerschmitt 210 test programme. Later, appointed Staffelkapitän of Erprobungsstaffel 210, he undertook night flying, anti-shipping and anti-invasion reconnaissance flights against England. These came to an abrupt halt when, on 6 September 1942, he had the misfortune in Messerschmitt 210 A-1, coded 2H+HA, to be intercepted by a Hawker Typhoon flown by Pilot Officer Bridges of No. 1 (Typhoon) Squadron, and both he and his Bordfunker, Feldwebel Rudolf Jansen, parachuted into captivity.

In October 1941 I. Gruppe, Schnellkampfgeschwader 210, detached from operational duties on the Russian front, started training/testing on the Me 210 A at Landsberg-Lech airfield. Training continued early in 1942, first at Lechfeld, and then at Tours in France. Given the wide range of flying abilities in the Gruppe, crash landings and deaths occurred. However the Gruppe was not fated to be equipped with the Me 210 at this time, and the ultimate outcome of all this was that they were re-equipped with Bf 110s and returned to the Russian front in late May 1942 as I. Gruppe, Zerstörergeschwader 1 to continue active service on that front. The return to the Russian front was not without incident for I. Gruppe, as three Bf 110 F-2s crashed during the transfer flights to the front. All the crashes were attributed to engine failure after take-off, and there was a suspicion that sabotage was involved on these machines. Each aircraft carried a member of groundcrew, and the loss of 9 personnel for 3. Staffel was hard, particularly as one was Staffelkapitän Oberleutnant Georg Boxhammer, a veteran of Battle of Britain days.

1942

On 4 January 1942 Schnellkampfgeschwader 210 was re-designated Zerstörergeschwader 1, the two Gruppen of Schnellkampfgeschwader 210 becoming the I. and II. Gruppen of the new unit, flying Bf 110s. III. Gruppe was formed from reconnaissance pilots and others fresh out of training schools, and was equipped with Bf 109 E-7 fighter-bombers.

Active service on the Russian front eventually followed with the inevitable losses in aircraft and crews. In the summer of 1942 III. Gruppe was detached from the Russian front and deployed to the Mediterranean area. On this front they suffered a particularly heavy loss on 1 September 1942 when Gruppenkommandeur Major Roland Borth was killed in action. In late 1942 the Bf 109 E-equipped III. Gruppe was disbanded, 8. Staffel becoming 5. Staffel, Schlachtgeschwader 2, and 9. Staffel forming 6. Staffel, Schlachtgeschwader 2. While this disbandment was taking place, a new III. Gruppe was being formed from elements of Kampfgeschwader 40 and Seeaufklärungsgruppe 128. This new III. Gruppe was equipped with the Messerschmitt 210 A-1 and carried the revised unit code of '2N', a reversion to the original code carried by the first Wespen aircraft at the outbreak of the war.

A IV. Gruppe came into existence at around the same time. 10. Staffel was formed in September 1942, later becoming NNJ Schwarm/ Luftflotte 4 in August 1943. An 11. Staffel was formed in October 1942 from 16./KG 6 (which evolved out of Erpr. St. 210). 11. Staffel's life in Zerstörergeschwader 1 was brief, as it became Erprobungsstaffel 410 from December 1942 flying Me 410s. For a short time 11. Staffel carried a unit code of '3E', as evidenced by the loss of '3E+NQ' on 13 November 1942. The use of 'Q' as a Staffel letter cannot be explained. However the Staffel soon reverted to more traditional standards – 29 November saw the loss of '2N+MV', which showed conformity with the unit code and correct Staffel letter. 12. Staffel was formed in October 1942, later becoming NNJ Schwarm Ost in May 1943. IV. Gruppe was equipped with the Messerschmitt 210 also.

The unit lost one Gruppenkommandeur, Hauptmann Rolf Kaldrack of II. Gruppe, and nine Staffelkapitäne during 1942.

1943

At the turn of the year, the Messerschmitt 110-equipped I. and II. Gruppen received the Bf 110 G-2 variant, and were soon showing this model in their loss lists. At this time these two Gruppen still carried the code 'S9'. The first time '2N' appears in a loss list for II. Gruppe was in January 1944; for I. Gruppe, February 1944, by which time I. Gruppe was equipped exclusively with Junkers 88 C-6s.

In the spring of 1943 II. Gruppe moved to Italy , operating out of Trapani, Pomigliano, Montecorvino and Pisa between April and July, before withdrawing to Istris and Lorient in France in August.

III. Gruppe, meanwhile, still operated in North Africa, and an example can be given of the unusual nature of the conflict in the desert between the respective ground forces by describing what happened to Obergefreiter Anton Hacker of 9. Staffel. Hacker, together with Obergefreiter Schlögl, was posted on guard duty for a crash-landed Me 210 15 Kilometres north-west of El Djem. On the morning of 9 April 1943 he left the aircraft and Schlögl to do a recce of the surrounding area to see if there were any enemy troops nearby. The next the unit heard about him was a report received in May 1943 that he was a prisoner – a passing British patrol had picked him up and taken him into captivity. The aircraft was later recovered by the unit. An example of the transient nature of the desert war, where opposing sides could pass close to each other without realising the others existence. In this case, a passing patrol easily took an enemy soldier prisoner, but missed the other guarding an aircraft.

III. Gruppe took the Messerschmitt 410 on charge briefly in the later months of 1943, and in October 1943 lost seven aircraft in combat in a matter of days. The Gruppe was soon re-mustered, and had become a Junkers 88 C-6-equipped unit in the following month. I. Gruppe took a similar path, the Bf 110 crews moving to I. Gruppe, Zerstörergeschwader 26, and 13., 14. and 15. Staffeln of Kampfgeschwader 40 being re-designated 1., 2. and 3. Staffeln respectively of I. Gruppe. These Junkers 88 C-6 crews of I. and III. Gruppen operated over the Bay of Biscay and the Atlantic searching for allied convoys as well as providing submarine escort. By this time the Allied air force was equipped with aircraft which were more than a match for the Junkers 88 C-6s, and Mosquitoes and Beaufighters took a continuous toll of the German machines. Because of the nature of the missions, survivors were rare when an aircraft was brought down over water, as the loss tables for these two Gruppen testify for late 1943 and on into 1944.

II. Gruppe followed the general German retreat from North Africa through Italy, and was eventually to find itself in France for a short time before arriving at Wels in Austria in November 1943, following a rather nomadic existence in the previous months. Wels became its base until Zerstörergeschwader 1 was disbanded in the middle of the following year. II. Gruppe was the only Gruppe of the unit to fly the Bf 110 from start to finish of its existence.

As ever, losses were suffered in commanding officers. In 1943 the unit lost in action its Geschwaderkommodore, Oberstleutnant Joachim Blechschmidt, and Gruppenkommandeure from I., II. and III. Gruppen.

1944

The start of 1944 saw the Luftwaffe heavily engaged in a defensive war on all fronts, with all Gruppen being actively involved: I. Gruppe, with Junkers 88 C-6s, operating in the Atlantic area; II. Gruppe with Bf 110 G-2s in Austria attempting to protect the southern area of the Reich, and III. Gruppe with Junkers 88 C-6s also over the Atlantic.

The bleak prospects for the crews of Zerstörergeschwader 1 in this year can be illustrated by the losses suffered as the months progressed. On 11 April 1944 I. Gruppe lost 17 men with 5 wounded; on 29 May II. Gruppe had 18 aircrew killed in action, with a further 7 wounded, and I. Gruppe suffered grievously again when the Allied invasion of Europe occurred on 6 June, with losses on 6 and 7 June of 26 lost and 5 wounded. Between 26 and 28 June II. Gruppe was again hard hit with 18 killed and 8 wounded.

A once proud fighting unit which had seen active service in almost every theatre of war the Luftwaffe was involved in now succumbed to the vagaries of re-organisation, and the famous 'Wespengeschwader' ceased to exist in early July 1944.

Photos

OPPOSITE:
Top: The original 'Wespe' emblem was carried on Bf 110s of II. Gruppe Zerstörergeschwader 1 in the early months of the war and consisted of three small wasps above clouds. That unit took the emblem with it when it was redesignated III. Gruppe, Zerstörergeschwader 76 in 1940. The emblem was designed by Leutnant Richard Marchfelder, the Technical Officer of the Gruppe, who was shot down into captivity over England on 16 August 1940.

Bottom: I. Wart Unteroffizier Adam stands before a Bf 110 E of I./Schnellkampfgeschwader 210 at Denain. The emblem first used by Erprobungsgruppe 210, the British Isles in a gunsight, was placed in a shield with a white background and black outline. Note the unusual positioning of the Werknummer, 3722, on the nose, and the armour protection for the pilot.

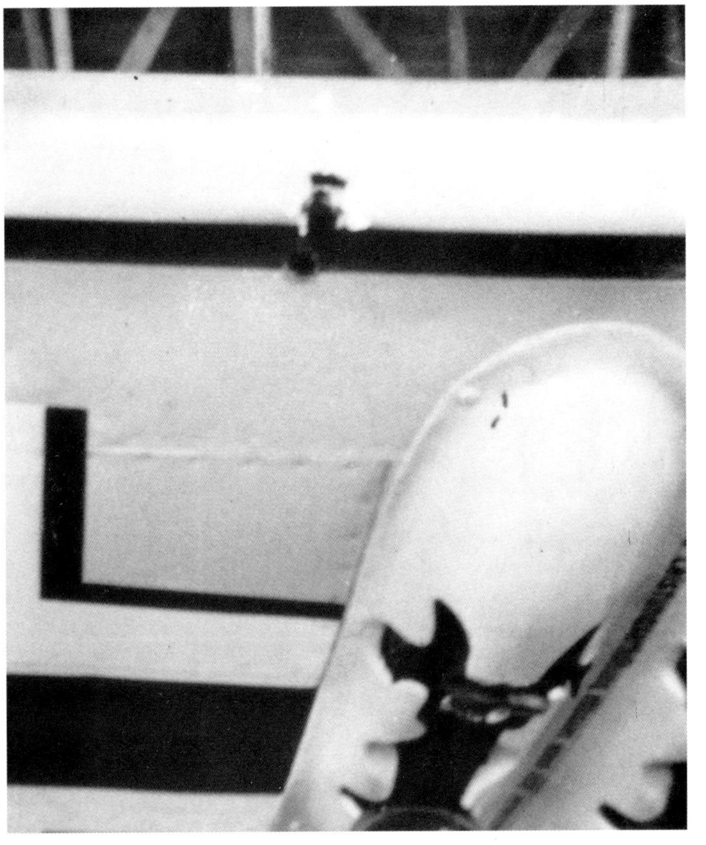

FOUR PHOTOS THIS PAGE.
Four views of the damage sustained by S9+ML of 3. Staffel, Schnellkampfgeschwader 210 on the evening of 7 May 1941 off the coast of Great Yarmouth. Pilot Unteroffizier Helmut Lußky managed to get back to base on one engine with his Bordfunker, Gefreiter Karl Schröder. Strikes can be seen on the wing, fuselage and fin.

Pilot Helmut Lußky, seen here later in the war as an Oberfeldwebel with his pilot's badge, Frontflugspange, Iron Cross 2nd Class ribbon and Iron Cross 1st Class clearly seen.

Karl-Fritz Schröder, Lußky's Bordfunker, in a later-war years pose wearing the ceremonial dolsch (dagger).

Five Unteroffiziere pose for the camera. From left: Natzinger; Schlömer; Engels; Wiese and Schlee. The event is the award of the Iron Cross, Second Class, to Engels. Natzinger and Schlee survived the war. The fate of Schlömer is not known. Helmut Engels, known as 'Bubi' because of his baby face, was posted missing in action on 12 May 1941 in Bf 110 E-1, S9+CK, W.Nr.3459, together with Gefreiter Adolf Knöckel and Rolf Schilleng. Herbert Wiese was killed in action at the start of the Russian campaign, on 23 June 1941, together with his pilot, Leutnant Walter Kloß, in Bf 110 E-2, S9+LK, W.Nr.4003. Note the Schnellkampfgeschwader 210 emblem in the form of a plaque on the wall.

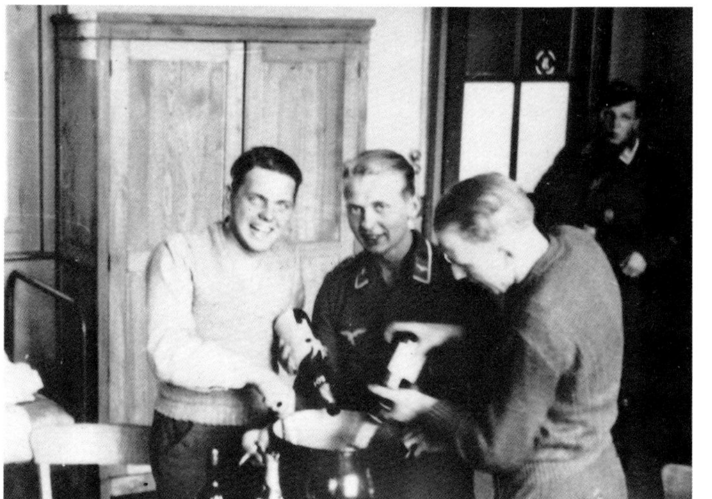

A lethal concoction of punch being prepared by, from left, Unteroffizier Rolf Schilleng, Unteroffizier Helmut Engels and Unteroffizier Gerhard Schlee, all of 2. Staffel.

2nd Staffel crew from Erprobungsgruppe 210 days: left is Feldwebel Johannes Claßen, pilot, with Feldwebel Willi Lukas, Bordfunker. Claßen was wounded in action on 22 June 1941 with Feldwebel Stephen Stadler in Bf 110 E-2, S9+GK, W.Nr.3796. Willi Lukas was killed on 14 September 1942 when the Bf 110E he was flying in, S9+KK, W.Nr.3996, collided with another aircraft while landing at Frohlof airfield.

Grave of Leutnant Erich Disper of 3. Staffel, Schnellkampfgeschwader 210, who was shot down by a Soviet fighter on 5 July 1941 in Bf 110 E-2, S9+CL, W.Nr.4406. The remains of S9+CL can be seen in the background.

In this later view of Disper's grave a replacement marker has been put in place, and the fuselage remains of S9+CL have been removed.

The two girls appear suitably impressed with what the young officer is telling them, while the other's attention is momentarily diverted to something in the cockpit. Part of the Schnellkampfgeschwader 210 emblem can just be seen in the bottom right corner of the photograph.

Left: 5. Staffel aircrew, from left: Feldwebel Kurt Jebramzik, pilot; Gefreiter Richter, Unteroffizier Georg Hemmetter, Bordfunker. Hemmetter and Jebramzik were posted missing in action on 27 July 1941 in Bf 110 E-2, S9+AN, W.Nr.4105.

Above: Bf 110, S9+AH of Wolfgang Schenck at Sechtschinskaja in September 1941. The fin carries 15 victory bars with the rudder sporting 5 tank 'kills'. Note the reversion to a thin white outline to the fuselage cross, and the theatre band forward of the Staffel letter 'H'.

Oberleutnant Forgatsch (centre) records a radio broadcast while Oberleutnant Brunzel, leaning against the tree, appears bored by the whole thing.

Left: Oberleutnant Heinz Forgatsch, Staffelkapitän of 3. Staffel, Schnellkampfgeschwader 210. Forgatsch had flown with 2. Staffel, Erprobungsgruppe 210 in 1940. He took over leadership of the Erprobungsstaffel 210 on 14 August 1941, and crashed to his death on 23 September 1941 in a Messerschmitt 210 A-1.

This photograph shows officers from I. Gruppe, Schnellkampfgeschwader 210. From left: Hauptmann Stricker; Leutnant Boxhammer; Oberleutnant Schenck; Hauptmann Diesing and Oberleutnant Forgatsch.

August 1941. Following the award of the Ritterkreuz, Oberleutnant Wolfgang Schenck, standing at the head of the tables, addresses personnel of 1. Staffel, Schnellkampfgeschwader 210.

Hauptmann Karl-Heinz Stricker, left, and his Bordfunker, Oberfeldwebel Karl Reiche. They were shot down on 13 September 1941 in Bf 110 E-2, S9+AB, W.Nr.4014. Stricker died that day; Reiche succumbed to his injuries 10 days later.

Karl-Heinz Stricker, right, discusses a matter with an unknown Oberleutnant in the summer sunshine.

The grave of Karl-Heinz Stricker.

In the background is the grave of Karl-Heinz Stricker. The two graves immediately in front with the simple white crosses are those of a 1. Staffel, Schnellkampfgeschwader 210 crew, Leutnant Arno Rampel, left, and Gefreiter Emil Pelikowski. Rampel and Pelikowski crashed on a non-combat flight on 1 September 1941 in Bf 110, S9+BH, W.Nr.4469.

Unteroffizier Jacobs in the cockpit of his Bf 110 with a ground mechanic in attendance.

The grave of Unteroffizier Hans Kleber at Tschaikowka, which shows his date of death as 24 October 1941. There is no record of this loss in the aircrew loss lists, so it is likely that he was groundcrew.

Below: In-flight view of two Bf 110s of Schnellkampfgeschwader 210 with the unit emblem showing on the nearest aircraft.

Crash-landed Bf 110 of 2. Staffel. Note the theatre band around the fuselage and the unit emblem. The upright propeller blade on the starboard engine would indicate that this Bf 110 came to earth with only the port engine functioning.

Facing the camera is Hauptmann Hermann Roth, Staffelkapitän of 5. Staffel, Schnellkampfgeschwader 210. He was killed in action on 6 November 1941 with his Bordfunker, Unteroffizier Heinz Berndsen, in Bf 110 E-2/Trop, S9+EN, W.Nr.4478, following a hit from anti-aircraft fire.

Tented quarters in the field carrying the Schnellkampfgeschwader 210 emblem.

1. Staffel, Schnellkampfgeschwader 210 quarters in Russia, which also shows the Field Post number of L25082.

3. Staffel, Schnellkampfgeschwader 210 entrance to field quarters at Seschtschinskaja, September 1941. The sign over the entrance says: "Uns geht die Sonne nicht unter", which roughly translates as: "The sun does not go down on us".

Loading bombs onto the central bomb rack of a Bf 110 E of the unit.

Right: The engines of this II. Gruppe Bf 110 C-6 are being run up. The muzzle of the 30 mm. MG 101 Kanone can be seen under the fuselage.

Although of poor quality, these two photographs show a Bf 110 sporting both the Schnellkampfgeschwader 210 badge and the large 'Wespe' which became synonymous with Zerstörergeschwader 1.

Excellent in-flight view of a Bf 110 E of the unit on the way to a target on the Russian front. The reason for only one bomb being carried is not known.

This Bf 110 D-3 is something of a mystery. By the time the unit code 2N was used on aircraft of the unit, they were flying Bf 110 G-2 day fighters. It is possible that this aircraft transferred with III. Gruppe, Zerstörergeschwader 76 to II. Gruppe, Schnellkampfgeschwader 210, and in the process retained its unit code for a time. III. Gruppe, Zerstörergeschwader 76 had retained II. Gruppe Stab and Staffel letters during 1940 and early 1941.

Another Bf 110 Wespe with the code 2N. The smaller size aperture for the engine oil cooler points to this being an early variant, and therefore possibly identical in circumstances to the previous aircraft.

Groundcrew receiving instruction on anti-personnel bombs in front of a Bf 110 of the unit.

This Bf 110 E carries an auxiliary fuel tank under the starboard wing and has an armoured windscreen.

This 'Wespe' emblem displays several differing features in the application of the emblem to that in the previous photograph, particularly in the areas of the wings and body.

Above: A weather-beaten Wespe emblem on a Bf 110 E stands out starkly against the snow-covered landscape of a Russian winter.
Opposite: Another winter view of a Bf 110 of the unit which will be the focus of attention for groundcrew. Note the wear on the propeller blades.

Crash-landed Wespe in the snows of a Russian winter. The pilot of S9+RM of 4. Staffel has brought his machine in to a relatively safe landing with the starboard engine on fire.

Two views of a Bf 110 E with an unknown crew posing on it while ground personnel work on the port engine. Of interest is the different spinner caps, and the two rectangular holes just forward of the bomb rack for the ejection of spent cartridge cases.

31 January 1942. Two views of the crashed Messerschmitt 210 A-1, NT+CX, W.Nr.080, of Oberfeldwebel Otto Rückert, who was killed in the crash at Landsberg.

31 January 1942 again. Two views of Unteroffizier Hans Tillheim's crashed Messerschmitt 210 A-1, GT+VH, W.Nr.090. This also occurred at Landsberg, and again the pilot was killed in the crash.

Engines are running, but no bombs are in evidence on the bomb rack of this Bf 110 E. Note the under-wing bomb racks, and the fact that the Wespe emblem and the swastika have been masked out while the white winter camouflage was applied.

Another snow-covered scene on a Zerstörergeschwader 1 airfield on the Russian front, with a Bf 110 C-6 prominently displaying the fairing for the 30 mm. MG 101 Kanone, and what appears to be a non standard gunsight on top of the fuselage. Despite the weathered look of the aircraft, the Wespe emblem seems to be in pristine condition.

One of the more unusual aspects of Luftwaffe armoury was the remotely-controlled rear firing machine guns, to pick off enemy aircraft trying to attack from behind. The guns were fired by the pilot in the Bf 110, not the Bordfunker. Although fitted as standard on the Messerschmitt 210 and 410, it was only used on an experimental basis with the Messerschmitt 110s of I. Gruppe. The idea came from Wolfgang Schenck, who wanted two 20 mm. cannon installed. He only received machine gun calibre weapons with which to carry out tests. In this photo, the 'periscope' attachment to the pilot's gunsight can be clearly seen in this winter scene.

S9+HH of 1. Staffel, another 'periscope' Bf 110, with the bulge in the fuselage visible from the base of the letter 'S' to the fuselage cross. Compare the thin white outline in the fuselage cross to that in the previous photograph.

Close-up of the nose of a Wespe. Note the armoured windscreen and the armour plate protection for the pilot attached to the seat. Note also heavy wear on the propeller blades, and the dented spinner.

Leutnant, later Hauptmann, Dominikus Kneidl, who flew with 8. Staffel of Zerstörergeschwader 1.

Feldwebel Sommer reports back after a milestone mission. Sommer had flown during the Battle of Britain with Erprobungsgruppe 210 with Bordfunker Gerhard Schlee. He was killed in action late in the war.

S9+FC of Stab, II. Gruppe, in a rather forlorn state.

Ground personnel laboured ceaselessly to keep serviceability states as high as possible. Seen here is Oberleutnant Kern of I. Gruppe, one of the officers responsible for ensuring the groundcrew kept the aircraft flying in all conditions.

Just inside the tented accommodation of 'Wespe 1' are various notices posted on a pole.

Two views of S9+PH of 1. Staffel, badly bent after a wheels-up landing.

S9+KM of 4. Staffel has lifting gear in place for an engine change on an unidentified airfield on the Russian front. The starboard engine, including propeller, has already been lifted from its wing mounting. The port engine and the fuselage from the rear cockpit to the nose has protective covers in place. Both S9+KM and S9+CM behind it have white propeller tips.

A mechanic works on the port engine of a Bf 110 which carries an armoured windscreen.

A Wespe Bf 110 shares a field with, from right, a Junkers 88 of II. Gruppe, Kampfgeschwader 76; a Junkers 88 of Kampfgeschwader 3, and a Henschel 129 of Schlachtgeschwader 1.

The port engine cowling is removed from this Wespe Bf 110 with bombs in the foreground and an auxiliary fuel tank in the middle distance.

Loading the bombs onto this Bf 110 has attracted a lot of interest. Note the very weather-beaten Wespe on the nose of this aircraft.

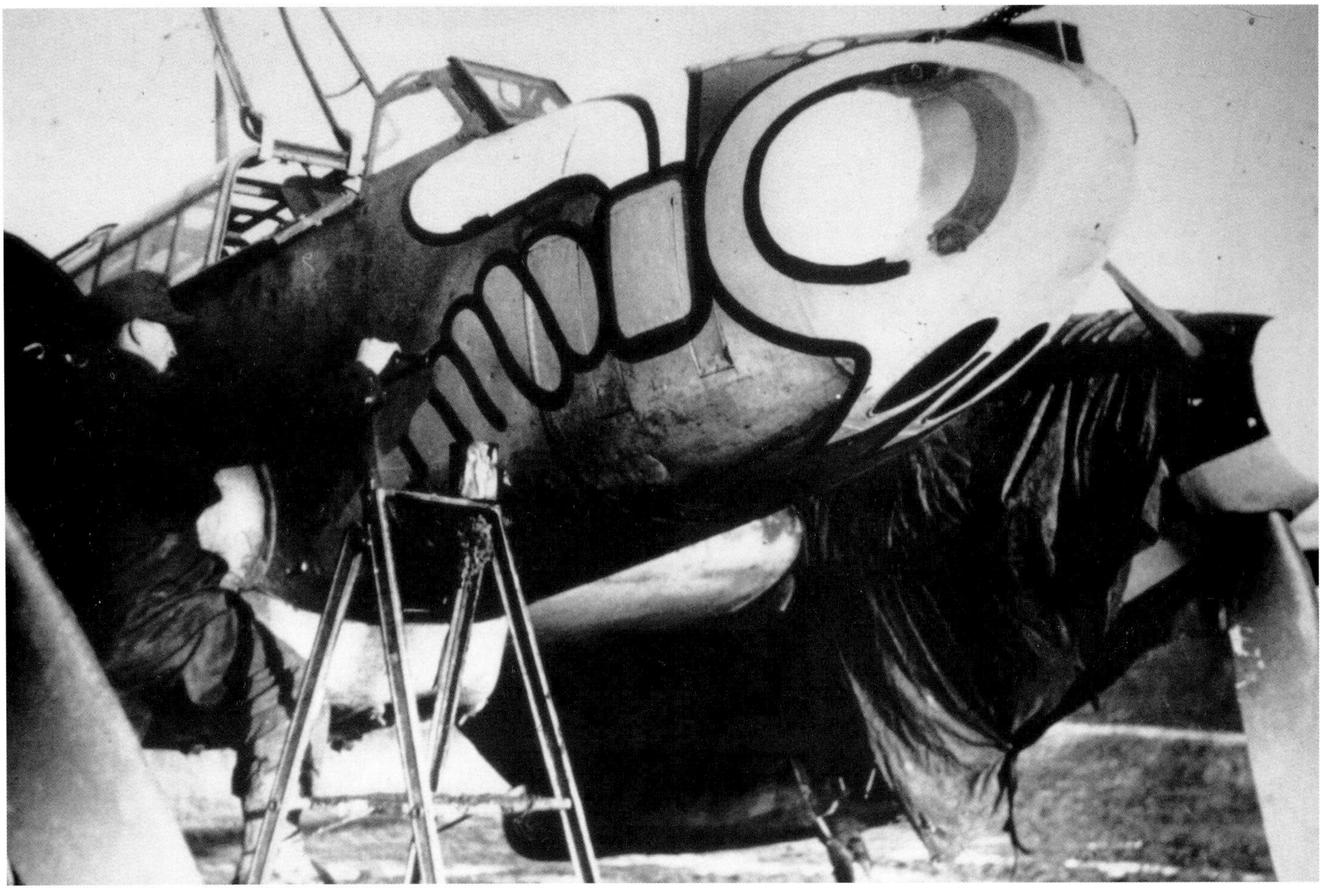

A groundcrew paints the 'Wespe' emblem on this Bf 110 E. Of interest are the multi-colored port spinner and the armour-plate on the windscreen. The bomb rack housing is in a far lighter color then the main undersurface of the aircraft.

A ground mechanic sits proudly on the cockpit sill of this Bf 110, which has a pristine Wespe on its nose.

A frequent occurrence at one time during the Russian campaign was the sight of the local population selling their wares on the airfields which the Luftwaffe occupied, as seen on this occasion on a Zerstörergeschwader 1 airfield.

Two ground personnel pose for the camera while the Bf 110 in the background is serviced. The theatre band on the fuselage appears to be behind the fuselage cross, very unusual for the Wespengeschwader.

Below: Taken from the Bordfunker position, this view shows four Bf 110s of the unit with ground personnel taking a break in the middle distance. The aircraft on the left does not carry the Wespe emblem, but appears to have the Schnellkampfgeschwader 210 emblem just forward of the cockpit.

The engines of this Wespe are run up by a ground mechanic.

Two views of Bf 110s showing to advantage how the bomb rack hinged downwards on the starboard side to allow access to the bomb release mechanism. Note the differences between the two Wespe emblems, particularly in the areas of the thickness of the body and the back sweep of the wings. Note also the rear view mirror on one of the Bf 110s.

S9+SN of 5. Staffel forms a backdrop for a gathering of personnel. On the extreme left of the group is Leutnant Erich Le Claire. Le Claire, of the Staff Flight of II. Gruppe, was killed in action on 8 January 1943 together with his Bordfunker, Feldwebel Ernst Frank of 4. Staffel, when their Bf 110 E-1, S9+JP, W.Nr.4493, received a direct hit from Flak while attacking a Russian airfield.

Close-up view of S9+SN of 5. Staffel with the rear fuselage jacked up during servicing.

A formal portrait of Leutnant Manfred Theves. He joined the unit at the start of 1942, eventually rising to the position of Staffelkapitän of 1. Staffel in 1944. He wears the Iron Cross Second Class ribbon, the Iron Cross First Class on his breast pocket, and above it the Frontflugspange.

Three in-flight views of 5. Staffel aircraft, with S9+TN nearest the camera.

Leutnant Claßen of Schnellkampfgeschwader 210 and Zerstörergeschwader 1. Of particular interest is the cloth emblem of Schnellkampfgeschwader 210 worn only by flying crews. The practise of carrying the unit emblem on clothing is believed to have been unique to this unit within the Luftwaffe.

Oberleutnant Georg Boxhammer, Staffelkapitän of 3. Staffel, Zerstörergeschwader 1. Boxhammer had flown with 1. Staffel, Erprobungsgruppe 210 as a young Leutnant, and had progressed through Schnellkampfgeschwader 210. He was killed when his Bf 110 F-2, S9+LL, W.Nr.4610, crashed on take-off from Krakau on 29 May 1942. The cause was believed to be port engine failure.

Unteroffizier Herbert Knef, Bordfunker, examines damage to S9+RK, while carrying apparent combat damage of his own. Knef was killed while flying with Boxhammer on 29 May 1942.

Unteroffizier Werner Gebhardt, Bordfunker of Leutnant Köhler, who died with his pilot on 11 June 1942.

Oberleutnant Kurt Seifert of 2. Staffel, posted missing in action on 3 June 1942 in Bf 110E, S9+SK, W.Nr.4355.

Unteroffizier Karl Gahleitner, Bordfunker of Oberleutnant Seifert. Gahleitner became a prisoner-of-war on 3 June 1943, but died in Soviet captivity on 26 July 1943.

Below: S9+AN, ostensibly the aircraft of the Staffelkapitän, with two bombs under the fuselage, moves off for another mission on the Russian front.

Three views of 5. Staffel Bf 110s in flight. None of these aircraft are carrying bombs on the bomb racks.

Leutnant Kurt Köhler of 2. Staffel, who was killed in action on 11 June 1942 in Bf 110, S9+BK, W.Nr.4089.

The grave of Leutnant Köhler and Unteroffizier Gebhardt.

Hauptmann Wolfgang Schenck is greeted on the completion of his 200th mission, June 1942. His Bordfunker, Jupp Kehren, stands on the wing root about to alight, while a member of the ground crew watches on. Note the heavy mottle on Schenck's Bf 110, and the victory markings on the fin.

Left: Schenck, left, Kehren, centre, and a third unknown pose for photographs.

Personnel line up to congratulate Hauptmann Schenck. Shaking hands with Schenck is Leutnant Hans Walter, who was killed in action on 20 September 1942 in Bf 110E, S9+FK, W.Nr.4490. Fourth from right is Leutnant Heinrich Dankworth, who was killed in action on 25 August 1942 flying Bf 110 F-2, S9+AB, W.Nr.2706. Note in this photograph, and the previous two, the cloth badge of Schnellkampfgeschwader 210 on the left breast of the tunics.

Above and below: Two further views of Schenck about to board his Bf 110, and a mechanic ready to assist with final preparations before take-off.

Hauptmann Schenck poses with his Bf 110 which carries a varied payload on its bomb rack.

Although of poor quality, this rare shot shows a Bf 109 E-7 of III. Gruppe which has crashed on the Russian front. The burnt out cockpit section, unit code, and fuselage theatre band can be seen.

Tented accommodation of Feldwebel Böckler and Gefreiter Meier of II. Gruppe, affectionately named 'Haus Mimi', on a Russian airfield.

Oberleutnant Eduard Tratt wearing the Ritterkreuz, which was awarded to him on 12 April 1942. Tratt had started the war as a Leutnant with 1. Staffel, Zerstörergeschwader 1, and flew with Erprobungsgruppe 210 during the Battle of Britain. His later career included spells with Schnellkampfgeschwader 210, Zerstörergeschwader 1, Zerstörergeschwader 26, and Erprobungskommando 25. On 11 October 1943 he was appointed Gruppenkommandeur of II. Gruppe, Zerstörergeschwader 26. On 22 February 1944 he was killed in action while flying with Zerstörergeschwader 26 in a Messerschmitt 410 A-1.

Left: An unknown Obergefreiter leads the way out of quarters occupied by 4. Staffel, Zerstörergeschwader 1. No attempt has been made to remove the Russian signs from the door. Right: 5. Staffel sign, again paying scant regard to the Russian sign remaining on the door.

A Schwarm of Bf 110s. The terrain would suggest Italy rather than the Russian front.

Feldwebel Paul Karwatka, pilot of 1. Staffel, who was shot down on 19 June 1942 while flying Bf 110 F-4, S9+IH, W.Nr.2712. He died later in captivity.

Unteroffizier Wilhelm Leewen, Bordfunker of Feldwebel Karwatka, who was also taken prisoner on 19 June 1942. Leewen's ultimate fate is not known.

3. Staffel in mid-1942. From left: Unteroffizier Lußky; Oberleutnant Meyer-Erlach (standing); Unteroffizier Schmidt; Unteroffizier Michelmann; Unteroffizier Baumeister; Unteroffizier Schröder; Unteroffizier Tögel (behind Schröder); Unteroffizier Melzheimer; unknown; Unteroffizier Schulz; unknown Leutnant (standing); Leutnant Bergmeister (standing); Unteroffizier Aust; Unteroffizier Bieber; unknown in light shirt behind Bieber; Unteroffizier Wünsche and Unteroffizier Olonczik. Of those identified in the photograph, only Meyer-Erlach, Schröder, Lußky and Wünsche survived the war.

Right: On 26 June 1942 Adolf Galland visited the unit, and he is seen here chatting with officers.

Unteroffizier Lothar Olonczik, Bordfunker with 3. Staffel. Olonczik was missing in action together with his pilot, Leutnant Gustav Bergmeister on 22 June 1942 in Bf 110, S9+GL, W.Nr.3829.

Unteroffizier Wilhelm Tögel successfully belly-landed his Bf 110 F-2 on 28 June 1942 near Bjelgorod III airfield. Note this aircraft carries both the Schnellkampfgeschwader 210 badge and Zerstörergeschwader 1 Wespe.

Right: S9+IN coming in to land with everything down. Note the different placement of the theatre band compared to the next photograph.

Groundcrew of 3. Staffel mill around a table with various items on it at Bjelgorod airfield, summer 1942.

II. Gruppe Wespe of the Staff Flight, S9+CC, with standard theatre marking on the rear fuselage. The 'C' would normally be the mount of the Technical Officer of the Gruppe.

Feldwebel Herbert Kutscha, pilot of 5. Staffel. He was awarded the Ritterkreuz on 24 September 1942, and survived the war, ending it as a Hauptmann with 22 confirmed victories.

Leutnant Kurt Scheffel, right, of 1. Staffel, celebrates the completion of his 200th mission.

Close up showing to good effect the unit code, fuselage cross, theatre band, aerials and retractable ladder for access to the port wing root. Note also what appears to be a heavier-than-normal calibre rearward firing gun.

Another view of Kurt Scheffel celebrating his 200th mission. The customary garland of flowers has been placed around his neck.

This photograph shows to good effect the twin boom crane used by the unit for replacing engines.

Ground personnel on parade with a Wespe Bf 110 in the background. There appears to be a cavalier attitude in the ranks towards listening to instructions.

A member of the ground crew is in attendance in the cockpit of this Bf 110 which has its starboard engine cowling removed for work on that engine.

Right: An unknown, pensive, member of the unit sits on a barrel with a Bf 110 in the background.

1 July 1942. 3. Staffel Bf 110 F-2s lined-up in preparation for another mission. The nearest aircraft is S9+KL, W.Nr.4096, flown by Feldwebel Lußky and Unteroffizier Schröder.

Left: Mission's-end for S9+KL. The aircraft received a direct hit from a Russian tank, and Lußky had to execute a very difficult forced-landing – flying with one wing heavy, Lußky had to use all his strength to keep the Bf 110 in the air as it gradually lost height. When low enough, he let the aircraft flip, and as it came back into a horizontal position he put it down. "Lußky saved my life", Karl Schröder commented at a Wespen reunion many years later. Right: Lußky, left, and Schröder pose before their Bf 110. Note the cloth Schnellkampfgeschwader 210 emblem on Schröder's flying jacket.

Above and opposite: Four excellent in-flight views of 6. Staffel aircraft. The lack of bombs under the fuselage would tend to indicate a non-combat flight, or the flight back from a bombing attack.

S9

S9 LP

A pensive-looking Oberleutnant Rüdiger Ossmann stands before a Bf 110 with upper and lower engine cowling panels removed. This Bf 110 does not carry the Wespe emblem on its nose.

Bf 110 Fs of 1. Staffel, Zerstörergeschwader 1. The multi-colored spinners are a carry-over from the days of the original Zerstörergeschwader 1 in 1939, and were carried during the re-designations to Erprobungsgruppe 210 and Schnellkampfgeschwader 210. The Schnellkampfgeschwader 210 emblem is carried, but not the Wespe.

Unteroffizier Ludwig Kastner, pilot of 6. Staffel, missing in action on 2 July 1942 with his Bordfunker, Unteroffizier Gerhard Losse, in Bf 110 E-2/U-4, S9+SP, W.Nr.3976. Both crew were killed by Russian partisans.

Unteroffizier Kurt Steenbock, Bordfunker with 4. Staffel. Steenbock was killed in action on 13 July 1942 in Bf 110 F-4, S9+EM, W.Nr.2722. His pilot. Leutnant Joachim Hacker, returned to the unit, but was posted missing in action on 2 September 1942 near Stalingrad.

Left: Crash-landed Wespe of Leutnant Heinz-Helmut Brandes on 14 August 1942 at Armawir.

This page and opposite: 13 July 1942, near Woroschilowgrad. Six views of the belly-landed 5. Staffel Bf 110, S9+EN, W.Nr.4054 of Oberfeldwebel Wilhelm Dibowski, pilot, and Unteroffizier Kurt Meier, Bordfunker, which was damaged by Flak while attacking Russian tanks. Both Dibowski and Meier survived the war.

S9
EN

An unknown pilot of 1. Staffel celebrates the completion of 100 missions in front of his mount, S9+FH, with his Bordfunker standing alongside. Ground personnel watch from the port wing root.

Oberfeldwebel Wilhelm Dibowski with, among other decorations, a marksman's lanyard prominent on his right side.

Kurt Meier, seen here with the later-war rank of Feldwebel.

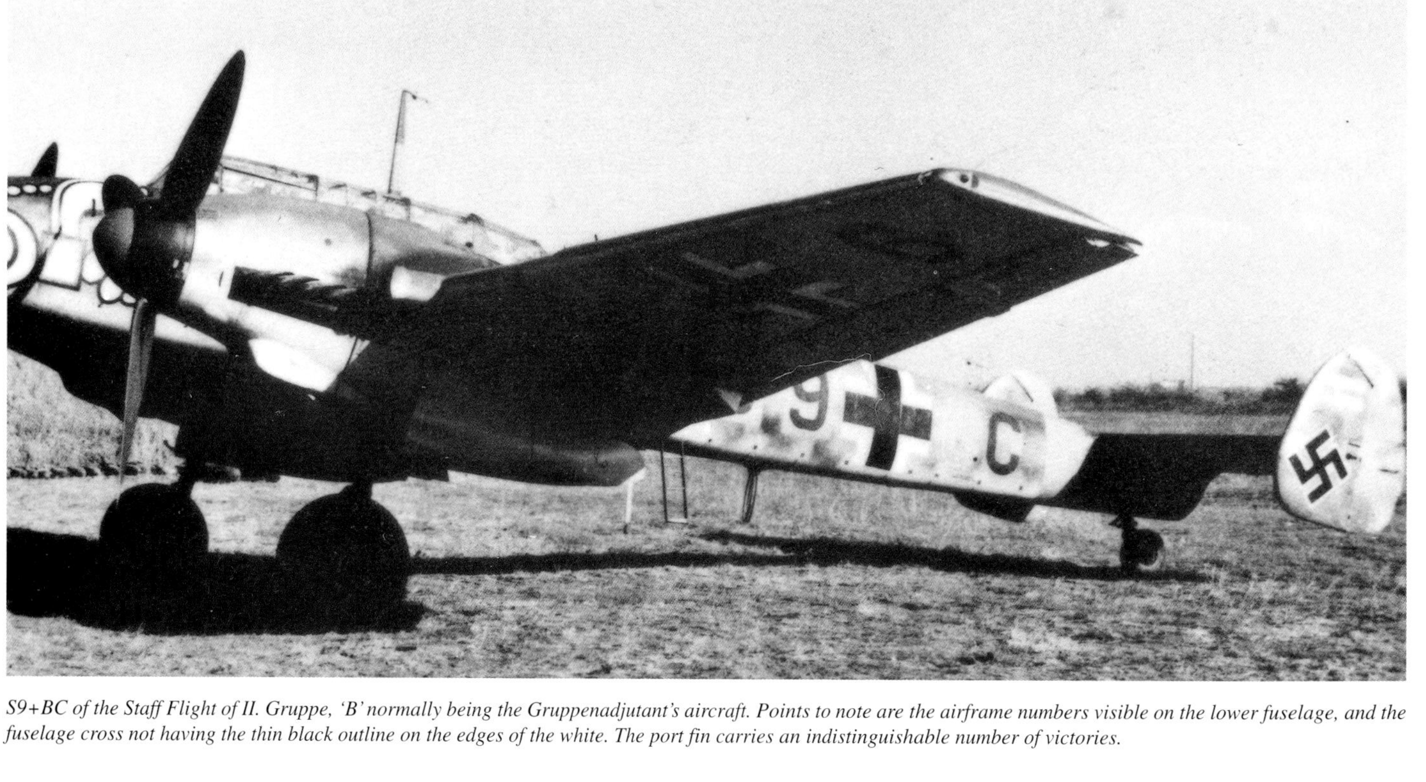

S9+BC of the Staff Flight of II. Gruppe, 'B' normally being the Gruppenadjutant's aircraft. Points to note are the airframe numbers visible on the lower fuselage, and the fuselage cross not having the thin black outline on the edges of the white. The port fin carries an indistinguishable number of victories.

Atmospheric photograph of Hauptmann Dominikus Kneidl, Staffelkapitän of 8. Staffel. Kneidl was posted missing in action on 22 July 1942 north-east of Rostov on the Russian front, in Bf 109 E-7, S9+LS, W.Nr.4212.

Leutnant Heinz-Helmut Brandes. After his spell with Zerstörergeschwader 1, he eventually moved to Jagdgeschwader 11, and was killed in action on 28 May 1944.

Excellent side-on view of S9+CN. The 'C' is yellow, outlined black. In the background is a Bf 109 E-7 of III. Gruppe, Zerstörergeschwader 1. The Wespe emblem can just be made out on its nose.

The Bordfunker of Oberleutnant Karl-Heinz Dzianowski of 6. Staffel congratulates him on the completion of his 150th mission.

Members of the unit display a placard announcing 150 'Feindflug' completed beneath a diving 'Wespe'.

S9+JH of 1. Staffel, with the major part of the forward section of the aircraft burnt-out. This may have been done for security reasons by the crew upon landing. There are no recorded crew losses against an aircraft with the code S9+JH.

Every unit had a photograph of a 'Flieger Denkmal', a flyers memorial, and the Wespengeschwader was no exception. Here, S9+CL of 3. Staffel stands ignominiously on its nose. What is somewhat unusual is that the letter 'S' is on the yellow fuselage theatre band; normally this yellow band was ahead of the 'S'.

An unknown member of the unit enjoys the sunshine of a Russian summer at the entrance to his tented living quarters.

Mechanics move bombs into position close by a Bf 110 which has covers on its port engine and nose.

Right: The openness of the Russian countryside can be clearly seen in this photograph of ground personnel relaxing near S9+AN. Note the underwing bomb racks inboard of the wing cross.

Below: The nearest Bf 110 has an auxiliary fuel tank on its bomb rack, indicating an overland or transfer flight rather than a bombing mission.

S9+HP of 6. Staffel has a smaller-than-standard white border on the fuselage cross. Also of note is the fact that this aircraft does not have the armoured windscreen or pilot's rear armour fitted. The aircraft letter 'H' is in the Staffel color of yellow, with a black outline.

An unknown crewman approaches S9+RP of 6. Staffel. Contrast the white border on the fuselage cross of this aircraft with that in the previous photograph. There is also a marked difference in the camouflage pattern applied to both these aircraft.

Dispersed Wespengeschwader Bf 110s on an unknown airfield on the Russian front.

A mechanic pauses from attending to a Bf 110 to pose for the camera as another aircraft in low flight passes on the starboard side. Note the inboard position of the pitot tube on the starboard wing. This would move to the wingtip on the 'G' series Bf 110.

Above left: Leutnant Otto Kempf, pilot of 1. Staffel, who was missing in action following combat with a Russian fighter on 11 August 1942 in Bf 110 F-2, S9+KH, W.Nr.2713. His Bordfunker, Unteroffizier Heinz Bothe, was also posted missing.

Above: Oberleutnant Kurt Schröder of 1. Staffel was killed in action on 11 August 1942 following combat with a Russian fighter in Bf 110 E-2, S9+OH, W.Nr.2649. His Bordfunker, Unteroffizier Karl-Günther Lämmel, was also killed.

Left: Feldwebel Adolf Gross, pilot of 1. Staffel, killed in action on 21 August 1942 in Bf 110 E-1, S9+SH, W.Nr.4064. Gross is seen here as an Unteroffizier, and sports the marksman's lanyard on his right side.

Opposite: Kuteinikowa, August 1942. Groundcrew work on both engines of this Wespe, which carries both armoured windscreen and pilot's armour. Note the capped spinner on the ground in the foreground.

Unteroffizier Friedrich Frese, Bordfunker of Feldwebel Adolf Gross, who was killed in action with his pilot on 21 August 1942.

Unteroffizier Georg Reuther, killed in action on 25 August 1942 with his pilot, Leutnant Heinrich Dankworth in Bf 110 F-2, S9+AB, W.Nr.2706.

Officers of 1. Staffel, Zerstörergeschwader 1 with reverse caps. From left: Oberleutnant Ossmann; Leutnant Theves; Leutnant Claßen. Note the Schnellkampfgeschwader 210 emblem on the side of the Arado 66.

An unknown pilot is greeted as he steps out of his Bf 110 F upon completion of a milestone number of missions. In the foreground the event is being recorded for posterity by another photographer.

S9+DR, W.Nr.4964, the mount of Unteroffizier Hans Sennholz. This 7. Staffel Bf 109 E-7 was brought down near El Alamein on 31 August 1942, Sennholz becoming a prisoner-of-war.

S9+EN of 5. Staffel forms a backdrop as an Oberleutnant completes 250 missions. Note on this machine the yellow theatre band is behind the third character of the fuselage code, 'E'.

All the required accoutrements are on view here as a Bf 110 undergoes an engine change.

Oberleutnant Helmut Viedebantt stands centre on the port wing root of a 5. Staffel Bf 110. Viedebantt became Staffelkapitän of 5. Staffel on 9 October 1942, and received the Ritterkreuz on 30 December 1942. He crashed to his death on 1 May 1945

Ground crew stand and watch as the engines are run up on S9+AM, a Bf 110 F of 4. Staffel. The fuel tank on the bomb rack would indicate a forthcoming overland or transfer flight.

Bf 110 F, S9+KM of 4. Staffel, again carrying a fuel tank on its bomb rack.

S9+CM, a Bf 110 F which has the same spinner markings as those in the previous two photographs.

An armourer works on the machine guns of a Bf 110 F which carries a gun camera in the nose.

Instructions being passed on from the rear of a Wespe Bf 110.

Armawir, September 1942. Ground crew bring two bombs to a Bf 110 E. In the background is Bf 110 E-2, S9+UN, W.Nr.2542, in which Unteroffizier Gottfried Seifert, pilot, and Unteroffizier Alfred Brandt, Bordfunker, were posted missing on 17 September 1942 after being rammed by a Russian fighter.

An unknown Oberfeldwebel of 5. Staffel stands alone with his thoughts beside his Bf 110, S9+GN. The 'G' appears to be red, outlined in black.

Feldwebel Danninger of 1. Staffel, seen here as an Unteroffizier.

The grave of Leutnant Karl-Heinz Heinelt of 5. Staffel. He was killed in action on 4 September 1942 in Bf 110 D-3, S9+KN, W.Nr.4346, north of Ssewerskaja. Heinelt's Bordfunker, Unteroffizier Otto Ehmann, was wounded, but survived the action.

The burial party fire a volley at Heinelt's graveside.

Above: Oberleutnant Robert Gebhardt, pilot of 3. Staffel. Gebhardt was killed in action on 18 September 1942 together with his Bordfunker, Feldwebel Karl-Heinz Menzel, in Bf 110E, S9+FL, W.Nr.4344.

Above right: Feldwebel Menzel, Bordfunker of Oberleutnant Gebhardt.

Right: Unteroffizier Richard Söchtig, missing in action on 19 September 1942 with his Bordfunker, Unteroffizier Heinrich Diemer, in Bf 110D, S9+PH, W.Nr.3713.

8th Staffel Bf 109 E-7, with the pilot in the cockpit and ground crew in attendance, which displays the Wespe emblem in its smaller form for Bf 109s.

Bf 109 E-7, S9+IS, W.Nr.6431, shot down on 2 October 1942 near El Alamein. The pilot, Leutnant Norbert Schmidt, was wounded. This Bf 109 carries sand overall upper surfaces, and the full Mediterranean theatre markings of white fuselage band, white wingtips and a white spinner.

Unteroffizier Hans Stoltenberg, Bordfunker of 1. Staffel, missing in action in the Stalingrad area on 23 November 1942 in Bf 110E, S9+TH, W.Nr.4008.

A New Year's greeting card from the Wespen-Geschwader 'from the East'.

Below: Messerschmitt 210 As of Zerstörergeschwader 1 in the Mediterranean theatre. All carry the white fuselage theatre band. Nearest the camera is DF+EH, yet to have unit codes applied. Behind it is 2N+ER. On the extreme left, the fourth character of the unit code is 'V', denoting an 11. Staffel machine. IV. Gruppe was only in existence for a short time towards the end of 1942, and it is therefore likely that this photograph dates between November and December 1942.

Oberleutnant Ossmann is carried shoulder-high from his Bf 110 G-2. Leutnant Theves is in the peaked cap.

The reason for the celebrations is shown on the card – Ossmann's completion of his 250th mission. His Bordfunker still has to make his way out of the aircraft. Note the revised, small, size of the letters of the unit code.

Another celebration for 1. Staffel. Left is Feldwebel Georg Müller, right, Oberleutnant Ossmann, with S9+GH behind them.

S9+GH forms a backdrop for a conversation between Leutnant Manfred Theves, left and Oberleutnant Ossmann.

Right: Stabsfeldwebel Paul Rapp of 4. Staffel. Rapp was killed making an emergency landing following combat on 11 July 1943 in Bf 110 G-2, S9+DM, W.Nr.6191. His Bordfunker, Feldwebel Gerhard Freyer, was uninjured in the crash.

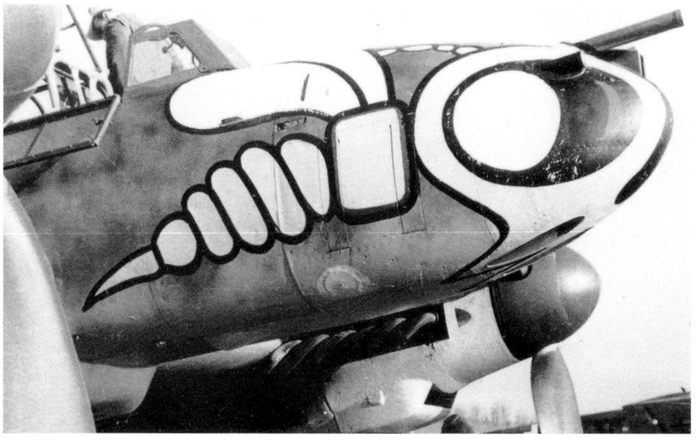

The front-end of a 5th Staffel Bf 110 G-2 showing the tubular back rest for the pilot, bolted-on armoured windscreen, and deep bath radiator.

Hauptmann Wilfried Hermann, Gruppenkommandeur of I. Gruppe, who was killed in action on 14 July 1943 with his Bordfunker, Oberfeldwebel Albert Weinhold in Bf 110 G-2, S9+FB, W.Nr.6327.

Major Joachim Blechschmidt, Geschwaderkommodore of Zerstörergeschwader 1, raises a bottle of Bols in celebration of an unknown occasion. The Ritterkreuz which he wears was awarded on 17 March 1943, and this photograph therefore dates between that date and 13 July 1943, when he was posted missing in action with his Bordfunker, Unteroffizier Hans Worl, in Bf 110 G-2, S9+BA, W.Nr.6295, after being shot down by a Yak 9 flown by French pilot, Albert Littolff.

View of the Bordfunker's position in a Bf 110 G-2. Note the twin MG 81 Z rear guns and associated gunsights. The W.Nr., 5243, can be seen in two places on a panel.

Two views of S9+CH, a Bf 110 G-2 of 1. Staffel. Note the color separation on the spinners.

Stripped-down Bf 110 G-2/Trop of II. Gruppe in the Mediterranean theatre. The flotsam and jetsam of retreat can be seen around the Bf 110, while in the background allied fighters now occupy a former Luftwaffe airstrip.

Two views of Leutnant Claßen, left, and his Bordfunker, Oberfeldwebel Schieder. Note again the small size of the unit code, and the lack of black surround on the fuselage cross.

A Bf 110 G-2 has the second bomb carefully set in place on a muddy airfield.

Junkers 88 C-6s of the unit take off from Bordeaux-Merignac airfield.

Unteroffizier Heinrich Bartling, Beobachter (Observer) with 7. Staffel, seen here in front of a Junkers 88 C-6 of the unit. He was killed in action on 20 November 1943 when his Junkers 88 C-6, 2N+GL, W.Nr.360403 was shot down in combat with British fighters.

This page and opposite: Five in-flight views of Junkers 88 C-6s of the unit. Of particular interest is the C-6 with single color camouflage over the fuselage, but with normal camouflage over the engine cowlings.

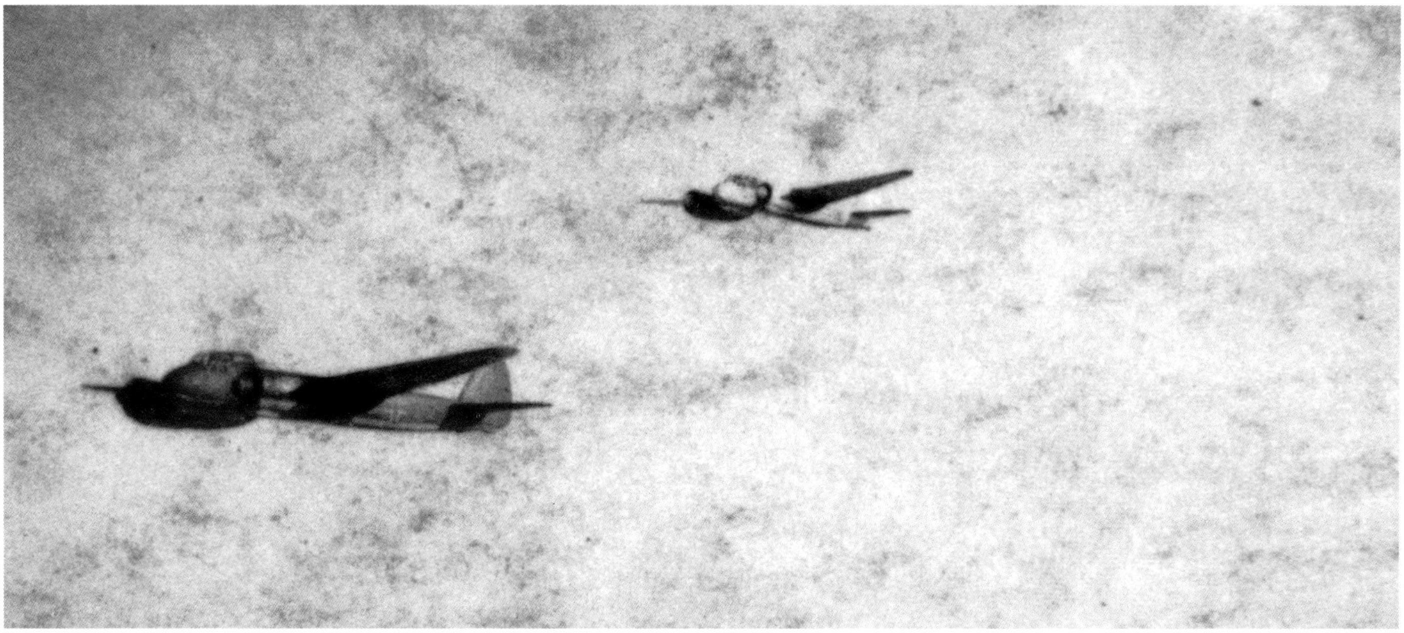

Feldwebel Otto Lusser, pilot with 7. Staffel, seen here in full flying gear. He was killed on a non-combat flight on 23 November 1943 when his Junkers 88 C-6 collided with another C-6 flown by Ofw. Erich Bindzus. Six members of 7. Staffel lost their lives as a result of this collision.

Gefreiter Rudolf Martin, Beobachter of 2. Staffel. He was posted missing in action in a Junkers 88 C-6 following an attack on a RAF Sunderland on 30 November 1943.

Bf 110 G-2 of the unit at Wels in Austria. This aircraft carries auxiliary fuel tanks under the wings and a ventral tray which housed two MG 151/20 cannon.

Two views of pre-mission activity for aircrew and Bf 110 G-2 machines of II. Gruppe. Note the small size unit code, used in the later-war period. Note also the W.Nr. on the top of the rudder, and the gap in the underside of the fuselage in the rear machine for the fitment of the ventral tray housing two cannon.

Well-known photograph, but nevertheless worthy of inclusion, of a Me 410 B-2/U-2/R-4 displaying a small size Wespe on the fuselage.

Edwin Hess in training at Kampfbeobachterschule Tutow, near Berlin.

2. Staffel Bordfunker, Obergefreiter Hermann Weissbrod, poses for the camera before a Junkers 88 C-6 at Vannes in March 1944.

5th April 1944. After a submarine escort mission, Junkers 88 C-6, 2N+FK, W.Nr.750411, overturned on landing at Vannes after rolling into a bomb crater. The crew of Reichelmann, Weissbrod and Hess survived.

Weissbrod's pilot, extreme right, Unteroffizier Hans Reichelmann, and Beobachter, Gefreiter Edwin Hess, third from right.

Below: III. Gruppe Junkers 88 C-6s flying low over the woods of Bordeaux. Note the light colored C-6 in the distance.

Leutnant Helmut Messerschmidt, pilot of 2. Staffel. He was posted missing in action on 11 April 1944 in a Junkers 88 C-6 following combat with Mosquitos.

Above right: Feldwebel Franz Hummel, Bordfunker of 4. Staffel, who was killed in action on 12 April 1944 in Bf 110 G-2, 2N+GM, W.Nr.6402, together with his pilot, Unteroffizier Walter Herkner.

Right: Feldwebel Herbert Oerzmann, pilot of 4. Staffel, who was killed in action on 12 April 1944 in Bf 110 G-2, 2N+KM, W.Nr.120045. His unknown Bordfunker survived the action.

In-flight view of four Bf 110 G-2s of II. Gruppe. The nearest aircraft carries auxiliary fuel tanks and Wfr. Gr. 21 rocket tubes under the wings, and what appears to be a ventral tray under the fuselage housing additional armament.

Unteroffizier Kurt Berns, Bordfunker with 7. Staffel, right, with two unknown members of III. Gruppe in front of a Junkers 88 C-6. Berns was posted missing in action on 20 April 1944.

Kurt Berns, seen here with the collar rank of Flieger.

Gefreiter Gerhard Körner, Beobachter, who was posted missing in action on 20 April 1944 in a Junkers 88 C-6 of 7. Staffel.

Head-on view of a Junkers 88 C-6 showing the gondola and nose armament offset to starboard.

Junkers 88 C-6 on the hard standing at Bordeaux-Merignac.

Oberleutnant Martin Reuter of 7. Staffel after alighting from his Junkers 88 C-6 on completion of a milestone mission for the Gruppe.

From Left, Hauptmann Morr, unknown, Leutnant Kurt Löw, all of III. Gruppe. Morr waits to greet Martin Reuter.

This page and opposite: Five in-flight views of Junkers 88 C-6s of III. Gruppe. Note again the light colored aircraft. The exact color is not known – it could be white, light blue or light grey. Note also the different colored tip to the fin and rudder.

Hauptmann Morr shakes hands with Reuter.

Above right and right: Two views of Reuter, now with a garland around his neck and surrounded by men of his unit.

Reuter is joined by an unknown member of his crew in the celebrations.

Above and above right: Two views of Oberleutnant Martin Reuter drinking a toast under the gondola of his Junkers 88 C-6, 2N+GR, with an unknown Leutnant of the unit. On 20 April 1944 Martin Reuter, Staffelkapitän of 7. Staffel, did not return from a combat mission together with his crew of Uffz. Friedrich Blumenröther, Bordfunker, and Unteroffizier Heinz Müller, Beobachter.

Right: Another view of one of Martin Reuter's crew, not standing on ceremony and swigging straight from the bottle!

Starboard undercarriage failure for this Bf 110 G-2 of the unit. Note the fuselage band and the code '2N' in small letters.

Bf 110 G-2 of II. Gruppe of the unit carrying underwing auxiliary fuel tanks.

Above: Gefreiter Hubert Licht (seen here as a Flieger), Beobachter of 8. Staffel. Licht was missing in action over the Mediterranean in a Junkers Ju 88 C-6 following combat on 11 May 1944. Unusually for this kind of aircraft loss, Licht's pilot, Uffz. Heinrich Lang was rescued from the sea.

Above right: Leutnant Kurt Löw of 7. Staffel, left, in flying kit. Löw was posted missing in action over the invasion front on 7 June 1944 in a Junkers 88 C-6, together with his crew of Unteroffizier Heinrich Seifert, Bordfunker, and Fahnenjunker-Feldwebel Gerhard Haberger, Beobachter.

Right: Unteroffizier Heinz Mayer of 5. Staffel, seen here as a Gefreiter. He was killed in action on 2 July 1944 in Bf 110 G-2, 2N+UN, W.Nr.6300 together with his pilot, Uffz. Horst Schumann, over Budapest. Schumann and Mayer were the last crew to be lost in combat by Zerstörergeschwader 1.

Bf 110 G-2 showing a pristine Wespe emblem but with oil streaks on the port engine panels.

Appendices

Appendix 1
Damage/Loss List

This damage/loss list is incomplete, as Quartermaster records are not available for the period January to July 1944.

SCHNELLKAMPFGESCHWADER 210 DAMAGE/LOSS LIST

Date	Name of crew and rank	Staffel	Status	Fate	Aircraft code & W.Nr.	Damage state	Reason for casualty	Place
01-05-41	Lt. Paul Drawe	2	P	K	Bf 110	100%	Crashed after dropping bomb on training flight.	Cazaux, west France.
07-05-41	Lt. Gustav Mejer Gefr. David Völkl	3 3	P Bf	M M	Bf 110 E-2 S9+KL 3793	100%	During combat with Hurricane received direct hit from AA fire and crashed.	Over the Channel.
07-05-41	Uffz. Helmut Lußky Gefr. Karl-Fritz Schröder	3 3	P Bf	W	Bf 110 S9+ML		Aircraft damaged on combat mission against shipping.	South-east coast of England.
09-05-41	Lt. Wolfgang Meyer-Erlach Gefr. Gerhard Wünsche	3 3	P Bf	W W	Bf 110 E-1 S9+GL 3817	100%	Combat with Defiant and fired at by AA. Both engines damaged. Crew baled out and landed near Dahem.	Near Merck.
09-05-41	Uffz. Johann Will Ogefr. Otto Rössler	5 5	P Bf	K K	Bf 110 E-2 3766		Crashed on landing.	Stavanger-Sola.
12-05-41	Uffz. Helmut Engels Gefr. Adolf Knöchel Uffz. Rolf Schilleng	2 2 2	P Bf Bs	M M M	Bf 110 E-1/N S9+CK 3459	100%	Did not return from combat mission to attack Martlesham Heath airfield.	North Sea.
12-05-41	Uffz. Albert Ernst Gefr. Hermann Lechler	3 3	P Bf	K K	Bf 110 E-1/N S9+AL 3484	100%	Combat mission against Ipswich. Both engines damaged by AA fire. Reached the French coast but crashed.	Bergnes, near Dunkirk.
15-05-41	Lt. Wolfgang Raffel Uffz. Johannes Goebel	1 1	P Bf	M M	Bf 110 E-1 S9+GH 3972	100%	Did not return from combat with Spitfires on raid on British shipping.	Channel.
19-05-41	Lt. Hans-Ulrich Hasse Uffz. Wilhelm Neumann	3 3	P Bf	PoW M	Bf 110 E-1 S9+BL 3483	100%	Did not return from combat mission against Lowestoft.	North Sea.
20-05-41	Oblt. Kurt Langhoff Ogefr. Martin Hausstein	3 3	P Bf	I I	Bf 110 E-1 3482		Belly-landing.	Lille.
30-05-41	Uffz. Helmut Möhlmann Gefr. Heinrich Dümpe	4 4	P Bf	K	Bf 110 D-3 4261	100%	Flying accident.	Near Münster-Handorf.
04-06-41	Uffz. Hans Tillheim Uffz. Harry Patzer	2 2	P Bf	I I	Bf 110 E-2 3782		Crashed on take-off.	Bretigny.
04-06-41	Fw. Hans Lindau	3	Bf	I	Bf 110 E-1 3819		Injured when aircraft made belly-landing.	Lippstadt.
04-06-41	Lt. Herbert Friesacher Gefr. Alexander Frauzen	Erg. St. 210 Erg. St. 210	P Bf	K K	Bf 110 E-1 3836		Crashed on training flight.	Merville.
17-06-41		II. Gruppe			Bf 110 E 4066	50%	Crash-landing.	Rogoznica airfield.
22-06-41	Fw. Johannes Claßen Fw. Stephan Stadler	2 2	P Bf	W W	Bf 110 E-2 S9+GK 3796	100%	Attack on Pinsk airfield. Right engine set on fire by Russian fighter. Crash-landed 15 Kms. west of Pinsk.	Pinsk.
22-06-41		Stab, I. Gruppe			Bf 110 E 3794	30%	Combat damage.	
22-06-41		Stab, I. Gruppe			Bf 110 E 3996	40%	Combat damage.	
22-06-41	Lt. Dieter Henzler Ogefr. Konrad Fassler	4 4	P Bf	M M	Bf 110 E-2 S9+FM 3767	100%	Did not return from combat mission.	Andrzejov.
22-06-41	Uffz. Willi Bach Ogefr. Gerhard Kretschmann	4 4	P Bf	M M	Bf 110 D-3 S9+LM 4291	100%	Did not return from combat mission.	Andrzejov.
22-06-41		4			Bf 110 F-2 3937	40%	Hit by Bf 110 E-1, W.Nr. 4064.	Rogoznica airfield.
22-06-41		6			Bf 110 E-1 4064	15%	Crashed into Bf 110 F-2, W.Nr. 3937.	Rogoznica airfield.
22-06-41	Fw. Richard Reinhold	6	P	K	Bf 110 E-1 3916		Killed when aircraft crash-landed after combat mission.	Rogozniczka.
22-06-41	Ofw. Hans Peterburs	6	P	W	Bf 110 D-3 S9+GP 4267		Wounded on combat mission.	Wysokie.
23-06-41	Lt. Walter Klöß Uffz. Herbert Wiese	2 2	P Bf	K K	Bf 110 E-2 S9+LK 4003	100%	Attack on Wolkowysk airfield. Hit by enemy fire and crashed.	4 Kms. north-west of Wolkowysk.
23-06-41	Lt. Werner Schwinning Ogefr. Ludwig Näder	4 4	P Bf	K K	Bf 110 E-1 S9+GM 3967	100%	Shot down on combat mission.	Bialki.

Date	Name of crew and rank	Staffel	Status	Fate	Aircraft code & W.Nr.	Damage state	Reason for casualty	Place
23-06-41	Ogefr. Hermann Riggert Ogefr. Heinz Trapp	5 5	P Bf	K W	Bf 110 D-3 4266		Overturned on landing following combat mission.	Labunki.
23-06-41	Uffz. Leo Schacht	5		K	Bf 110 D-3 4263		Killed in crash-landing following combat mission.	Rogezniczka.
23-06-41	Ofw. Ernst Wagner Uffz. Kurt Walter	6 6	P Bf	K K	Bf 110 D-3 S9+GP 4267	100%	Shot down on combat mission.	Bialystok.
23-06-41		Stab, II. Gruppe			Bf 110 F 2382	40%	Belly-landing following combat damage.	Near Brest-Litowsk.
24-06-41	Lt. Fritz von Sauer Ofw. Josef Hanzlick	1 1	P Bf	K K	Bf 110 E-2 S9+NH 3795	100%	Shot down by Russian fighter on combat mission.	Slonim.
24-06-41	Lt. Kurt Flak	I. Gruppe			Bf 110 E 3455	100%	Hit by Flak.	Radzyn.
24-06-41		I. Gruppe			Bf 110 E 4044	30%	Combat damage.	
25-06-41		I. Gruppe			Bf 110 E 3821	90%	Emergency landing.	Near Slonim.
25-06-42		I. Gruppe			Bf 110 E 4004	90%	Emergency landing.	Bialystok.
25-06-41	Lt. Fritz Fromme Gefr. Karl Nielsen	5 5	P Bf	K K	Bf 110 D-3 S9+JN 3716	100%	Shot down on combat mission.	West of Macibow, near Wolkowysk.
25-06-41		II. Gruppe			Bf 110 E 3771	45%	Crash-landing.	Rogozniczka.
26-06-41	Lt. Karl-Heinz Wildies Gefr. Alwin Stäb	2 2	P Bf	 K	Bf 110 E-2 S9+BK 4414	100%	Crash-landing. Crew got away from aircraft and were being fired at by Russian troops. Stäb lost from sight and killed.	Baranowitschi.
28-06-41		4			Bf 110 E 3935	60%	Belly-landing following combat damage.	Przewokl.
29-06-41		1			Bf 110 E-1/N 3969	60%	Airframe damage.	Retzin.
29-06-41	Oblt. Friedrich Amende (Staffelkapitän) Uffz. Alfred Leubner	2 2	P Bf	M M	Bf 110 E-2 S9+MK 3787	100%	Did not return from armed reconnaissance mission.	Not known.
29-06-41		4			Bf 110 E 3460	80%	Crash-landing.	Usedom.
30-06-41		2			Bf 110 E-2/N S9+KK 4008	100%	Emergency landing following hit from Flak.	Wodzimierz.
30-06-41	Fw. Kurt Böhm Uffz. Hans Dorner	4 4	P Bf	K W	Bf 110 D-3 3942	100%	Shot down on combat mission. Both crewmen baled out.	Bolschow.
30-06-41	Lt. Kurt Püttner	4	P	K	Bf 110 D-3 4385		Killed on combat mission.	Near Kalisch.
01-07-41	Ofw. Hermann Brennicke Gefr. Heinrich Mitnacht	1 1	P Bf	 K	Bf 110 E-2 S9+EH 3785	100%	Shot down by two I-15 fighters after attack on Trembowla airfield. Right engine hit.	South of Tarnapol.
01-07-41	Oblt. Fritz Plank Uffz. Paul Stawitzki	Gesch. Stab Gesch. Stab	P Bf	W W	Bf 110 S9+DA 4062		Aircraft hit by AA fire.	Letczany.
01-07-41		2			Bf 110 E-1/N 2377	100%	Hit by Flak.	Near Ostymo.
03-07-41		5			Bf 110 E-2 3777	30%	Damaged while taxi-ing.	Klemensow.
03-07-41		2			Bf 110 E 3471	15%	Crash-landing.	Matschulitsche.
05-07-41	Lt. Erich Disper Uffz. Ulrich Herrmann	3 3	P Bf	K K	Bf 110 E-2 S9+CL 4406	100%	Shot down by Russian fighter on mission against enemy airfield.	5 Kms. south of Orscha.
06-07-41		6			Bf 110 C-4 2138	30%	Crash-landing.	Mocznas-Zaze.
08-07-41		Stab, I. Gruppe			Bf 110 E 3856	45%	Emergency landing following hit from Flak.	Near Gritzkowitsche.
09-07-41		1			Bf 110 E 4024	45%	Belly-landing following damage in combat.	Near Pomisewje.
10-07-41	Uffz. Fritz Dornbracht Gefr. Rudolf Haupt	5 5	P Bf	W W	Bf 110 D-0 4360		Both crewmen wounded on combat mission.	8 Kms. south-east of Bobr.
10-07-41		5			Bf 110 E 3994	75%	Emergency landing following combat damage.	Bogary.
11-07-41		6			Bf 110 C-4 3071	70%	Damaged in combat.	Bogary.
15-07-41		4			Bf 110 E 3434	25%	Crash-landing.	Orscha.
15-07-41	Lt. Reginald Klenke Ofw. Walter Breiholz	5 5	P Bf	K K	Bf 110 E-2 S9+DN 3775	100%	Shot down by DB 3 on combat mission.	Near Schumyatschi.
15-07-41	Lt. Carl Haberlah Ogefr. Hans Hollburg	4 4	P Bf	M M	Bf 110 D-3 S9+FM 4353	100%	Did not return from combat mission.	Near Smolensk.

Date	Name of crew and rank	Staffel	Status	Fate	Aircraft code & W.Nr.	Damage state	Reason for casualty	Place
16-07-41		3			Bf 110 E 4407	30%	Airframe damage.	Orscha.
16-07-41	Gefr. Johannes Puchta	6	Bf	W	Bf 110 D-3 S9+LP 3718		Wounded on combat mission.	Orscha.
19-07-41	Fw. Wilhelm Sommer	2	P	W	Bf 110 E-2 KC+US 4389		Crashed on transport flight.	15 Kms. south of Minsk.
19-07-41		2			Bf 110 E 4406	90%	Crash-landed.	Near Minsk.
20-07-41	Oblt. Kurt Jacobs Fw. Friedrich Gruppe	Gesch. Stab Gesch Stab	P Bf	K K	Bf 110 S9+BA 4011	100%	Direct hit from Flak during attack on Wypolsowa airfield.	Wypolsowa.
20-07-41	Lt. Walter Hahn	Ln. Komp. SKG 210	Bf	W			Wounded on combat mission.	Roslawl.
20-07-41	Lt. Rüdiger Ossmann Gefr. Georg Müller	1 1	P Bf	W W	Bf 110 E-2 S9+DH 4021		Engine damage caused crash.	South of Tenkewe.
20-07-41		4			Bf 110 E 4070	50%	Damaged in combat.	Krasny.
22-07-41	Lt. Joachim Hertel Gefr. Hubert Schmitz	1 1	P Bf	M M	Bf 110 E-2 S9+DH 4438	100%	Engine hit during attack on Russian troops. Schmitz died in Jelabuga PoW camp on 26-02-42.	South of Dorogobush.
22-07-41	Uffz. Franz Moldaschl Ogefr. Gerhard Reichel	5 5	P Bf	M M	Bf 110 E-2 S9+EN 4489	100%	Did not return from attack on enemy troops.	30 Kms. south of Jeljnja.
23-07-41		5			Bf 110 E 3781		Crash-landing.	Orscha.
23-07-41		6			Bf 110 E 3978	60%	Belly-landing following combat.	Ljady.
25-07-41	Lt. Robert Mautner Gefr. Adolf Schapke	4 4	P Bf	M M	Bf 110 E-2 S9+EM 4484	100%	Did not return from combat mission.	Near Bryansk.
26-07-41	Uffz. Alfred Koch Uffz. Horst Sieland	2 2	P Bf		Bf 110 E-1 S9+DK 4095	100%	Shot down on attack on Bryansk airfield. Both crew returned to unit.	Near Bryansk.
26-07-41		2			Bf 110 C 4090	50%	Crash-landing following combat.	Near Schatalowka.
27-07-41	Uffz. Georg Hemmetter Fw. Kurt Jebramzik	5 5	P Bf	M M	Bf 110 E-2 S9+AN 4105	100%	Did not return from combat mission.	8 Kms. east of Kamjenjetz.
28-07-41	Fw. Heinrich Kücke Uffz. Johann Guse	1 1	P Bf	M M	Bf 110 E-2 S9+EH 4443	100%	Did not return from combat mission against Wjasma airfield.	South of Mitina.
28-07-41	Uffz. Arthur Luttringer Gefr. Wilhelm Keim	1 1	P Bf	M PoW	Bf 110 E-2 S9+GH 4465	100%	Did not return from combat mission against Wjasma airfield. Keim died in captivity on 29/6/42.	10 Kms. west of Mitina.
28-07-41	Lt. Ernst Hackbeil Ofw. Werner Martin	3 3	P Bf	M M	Bf 110 E-1 S9+HL 3980	100%	Did not return from combat mission against Russian AA guns.	Jermolino.
28-07-41		3			Bf 110 C 2381	100%	Belly-landing following hit from Flak.	Waskowo.
29-07-41	Ogefr. Karl Derler	5	Bf	W	Bf 110		Wounded on combat mission.	35 Kms. north-west of Roslawl.
29-07-41	Uffz. Günther Neumann Ogefr. Werner Hauer	5 5	P Bf	W W	Bf 110 E-2 3770		Both crewmen wounded on combat mission.	Cap Nowa.
30-07-41	Ofw. Karl Stütz Fw. Heinz Filsinger	1 1	P Bf	K K	Bf 110 E-1 S9+IH 3469	100%	Did not return from attack on Russian tanks.	15 Kms. south-west of Schatalowka airfield.
03-08-41	Fw. Gerhard Saretzki Ogefr. Heinz Schulte	1 1	P Bf		Bf 110 E-2 S9+FH 4452	100%	Shot down on combat mission. Both crewmen returned to unit.	Pridnepowskaja.
04-08-41	Lt. Werner Fritzsche Gefr. Klaus Hruschka	3 3	P	M M	Bf 110 CD+MO 4496	100%	Missing on ferry flight after taking off from Radzyn.	Believed to be Orscha-Minsk.
04-08-41	Fw. Max Edenburg	3	Bf	W	Bf 110 E 3445	35%	Crash-landing.	Schatalowka-Ost airfield.
07-08-41		1			Bf 110 E-2 3789	50%	Belly-landing.	Near Roslawl.
09-08-41		4			Bf 110 E-2 3768	30%	Damaged while taxi-ing.	Allenstein.
10-08-41		4			Bf 110 E-2 3782	40%	Crash-landing.	Malezino.
10-08-41	Ofw. Ludwig Mergard	5	P	W	Bf 110 E-2/Trop S9+DN 4450		Damaged on combat mission.	West of Nowgorod.
11-08-41		5			Bf 110 E-2/Trop 4485	90%	Emergency landing.	Near Dno.
12-08-41	Lt. Hans Hesse Gefr. Johannes Droramczik	2 2	P Bf	W W	Bf 110 E-1 S9+CK 4049		Damaged on combat mission.	Propajak.

Date	Name of crew and rank	Staffel	Status	Fate	Aircraft code & W.Nr.	Damage state	Reason for casualty	Place
12-08-41		2			Bf 110 E 2427	100%	Belly-landing.	Near Wrjetsch.
12-08-41		2			Bf 110 E 4480	70%	Combat damage.	Schatalowka-Ost airfield.
14-08-41	Oblt. Fritz Andres (Staffelkapitän) Uffz. Karl Pietzsch	2 2	P Bf	K K	Bf 110 E-2 S9+AK) 2376	100%	Received direct hit from Flak on combat mission to Jelnja.	5 Kms. west of Kassikowa.
14-08-41	Oblt. Günther Schmidt (Staffelkapitän) Uffz. Josef Sorgnitt	5 5	P Bf	M M	Bf 110 E-2 S9+BN 3772	100%	Did not return from combat mission.	6 Kms. north-east of Nowgorod.
20-08-41	Lt. Wilfried Erhard Gefr. Gerhard Zimmer	5 5	P Bf	K K	Bf 110 E-2 S9+FN 3765	100%	Did not return from combat mission.	16 Kms. north-west of Tschudowo.
22-08-41	Lt. Willi Heistermann Gefr. Hans Grimsmann	1 1	P Bf	K K	Bf 110 E-2 S9+BH 3798	100%	Crashed on combat mission.	Grasdowo.
22-08-41		4			Bf 110 E-2 4063	70%	Emergency landing.	Near Dno.
23-08-41		1			Bf 110 E-2 4497	100%	Shot down by fighters. Crew returned to unit.	
23-08-41		3			Bf 110 E 3822	20%	Belly-landing.	Witebsk.
24-08-41	Uffz. Alfred Behrendt Gefr. Hans Sachs	6 6	P Bf	M M	Bf 110 D-3 S9+LP 3718	100%	Shot down by Russian I-18 fighter.	3 Kms. south of Winy Russl.
24-08-41	Lt. Harry Wiesner Ogefr. Wolfgang Myrrhe	4 4	P Bf	M M	Bf 110 E-2 S9+EM 4106	100%	Did not return from combat mission.	East-south-east of Nowgorod.
25-08-41					Bf 110 E-1 S9+HP 4109	15%	Damaged in fighter attack.	Maletino airfield.
27-08-41	Lt. Hubertus Huy Gefr. Walter Förstl	4 4	P Bf	W W	Bf 110 E-2 S9+AP 3753		Damaged on combat mission.	1Km. south-east of Ljuban.
28-08-41		2			Bf 110 E 4468	30%	Damaged while taxi-ing.	Seschtschinskaja.
29-08-41	Oblt. Karl-Heinrich Matern	Stab, II. Gruppe	P	W	Bf 110 E-1 S9+IC 4057		Wounded on combat mission.	South of Lake Ladoga.
29-08-41	Uffz. Günther Neumann Gefr. Rudolf Haupt	5 5	P Bf		Bf 110 D-2 S9+KN 3402	100%	Shot down on combat mission. Both crewmen returned to unit.	
30-08-41					Caudron C445	20%	Hit by Flak.	Smolensk.
01-09-41	Lt. Arno Rampfel Gefr. Emil Pelikowski	1 1	P Bf	K K	Bf 110 S9+BH 4469	100%	Non-combat flight. Crashed flying on one engine.	15 Kms. north of Seschtschinskaja.
06-09-41		5			Bf 110 E-1 4912	40%	Bombing attack.	Seschtschinskaja.
11-09-41		2			Bf 110 E 4108	70%	Belly-landing following combat damage.	Near Seschtschinskaja.
13-09-41	Hptm. Karl-Heinz Stricker (Gruppenkommandeur) Ofw. Karl Reiche	Stab, I. Gruppe Stab, I. Gruppe	P Bf	K K	Bf 110 E-2 S9+AB 4014	100%	Both engines hit on combat mission. Crashed into woods. Reiche died on 23/9/41.	4 Kms. north of Akkulitschi railway station.
13-09-41	Ofw. Hermann Brennicke Ogefr. Heinz Laurentsch	Stab, I. Gruppe			Bf 110 E-2 S9+CH 4449	100%	No other details available.	
14-09-41	Uffz. Gerhard Schilcher Gefr. Robert Müller	5 5	P Bf	M M	Bf 110 E-2 S9+AN 4499	100%	Crash-landed behind Russian lines on combat mission.	85 Kms. north of Nowgorod.
17-09-41		3			Bf 110 E 3784	100%	Belly-landing following combat.	Near Siluki.
23-09-41	Oblt. Heinz Forgatsch (Staffelkapitän) Fw. Kurt Hoffmann	Erpr. St. 210 Erpr. St. 210	P Bf	K K	Me 210 A-1 0117	100%	Crashed on training flight due to engine damage.	Rechlin airfield.
30-09-41	Gefr. Ernst-August Bennemann Gefr. Martin Laukemann Ogefr. Helmuth Bräuer	4 4 4	P Bf I. Wart	K K K	Bf 110 E-1 S9+KM 3990		Crashed on non-combat flight.	Semionowka.
02-10-41	Oblt. Wolfgang Unbehaun Ofw. Heinz Schmidt	5 5	P Bf	K K	Bf 110 E-2 S9+KN 4487	100%	Shot down on combat mission.	South-east of Roslawl.
06-10-41	Lt. Heinz Klug Gefr. Herbert Hilsberg	4 4	P Bf	M M	Bf 110 E-2 S9+HM 4399	100%	Did not return from combat mission.	Russanowa, 10 Kms. east of Roslawl.
12-10-41	Uffz. Hans Beck Uffz. Otto Weissflog	6 6	P Bf		Bf 110 D-3 S9+MP 3719	100%	Both crewmen returned to unit after being shot down	Medyn. on combat mission.
12-10-41	Uffz. Arnulf Martin Gefr. Karl Stahl	6 6	P Bf	K K	Bf 110 E-2 S9+EP 3788	100%	Shot down by Russian AA fire.	18 Kms. east of Medyn.

Date	Name of crew and rank	Staffel	Status	Fate	Aircraft code & W.Nr.	Damage state	Reason for casualty	Place
18-10-41	Lt. Adalbert Kuhlmann Ofw. Hans Siebold	4 4	P Bf	K K	Bf 110 C-6 S9+AM 2254	100%	Did not return from combat mission.	25 Kms. west-south-west of Moscow.
22-10-41	Uffz. Günther Neumann Ogefr. Werner Hauer	5 5	P Bf	M M	Bf 110 E-2 S9+DN 4390	100%	Hit by Russian AA fire on combat mission.	25 Kms. south-west of Podolsk.
24-10-41		Erg. St. SKG 210			Bf 110 E-2 4391	20%	Emergency landing due to engine damage.	Near Sittard.
27-10-41		Erpr. St. 210			Me 210 A-1 116	100%	Crashed on airfield.	Rechlin airfield.
28-10-41	Lt. Horst Fischer Uffz. Franz Maurer	4 4	P Bf	M M	Bf 110 E-2 S9+AM 4460	100%	Did not return from combat mission.	10 Kms. south of Serpuchow.
28-10-41		6			Bf 110 D-3 4268	20%	Damaged while taxi-ing.	Orel-West airfield.
31-10-41	Gefr. Josef Mayr Gefr. Klaus Schulze	Gesch. Stab Gesch Stab	P Bf	W W	Bf 110 E-1 S9+DA 3889	100%	Shot down by Russian Flak. Both crewmen returned to unit 8 days later.	Tula.
31-10-41		I. Gruppe			Me 210 A-1 2252	35%	Belly-landing.	Landsberg-Lech airfield.
02-11-41		6			Bf 110 E-1 S9+MN 3786	25%	Damaged in combat.	Schaikowska.
03-11-41		I. Gruppe			Me 210 A-1 2257	15%	Undercarriage failure.	Landsberg-Lech airfield.
05-11-41		Gesch. Stab			Bf 110 E 3451	40%	Aborted take-off.	Orel airfield.
06-11-41	Hptm. Hermann Roth (Staffelkapitän) Uffz. Heinz Berndsen	5 5	P Bf	K K	Bf 110 E-2/ Trop S9+EN 4478	100%	Shot down by Russian AA fire.	Usslowaja, 40 Kms. east of Tula.
13-11-42		5			Bf 110 E-2 4518	40%	Belly-landing.	Orel airfield.
28-11-41	Oblt. Hermann Smend Fw. Hubert Schulz	4 4	P Bf	W W	Bf 110 E-2 S9+FM 4525	100%	Shot down on combat mission.	25 Kms. north-west of Krapiwna.
05-12-41		I. Gruppe			Me 210 A-1 2260	70%		Landsberg-Lech airfield.
06-12-41		I. Gruppe			Me 210 A-1 2256	20%	Belly-landing due to technical failure.	Landsberg-Lech airfield.
06-12-41	Lt. Wolfgang Meyer-Erlach Gefr. Karl-Fritz Schröder	3 3	P Bf		Me 210 A-1 S9+CL 2258	20%	Damage to cockpit during flight.	Landsberg-Lech airfield.
08-12-41	Fw. Friedrich Carlsen Gefr. Karl Schneider	Erg. St. 210 Erg. St. 210	P Bf	K K	Bf 110 E-2 4012	100%	Crashed on training flight.	Merville.
09-12-41	Oblt. Helmut Lolhöffel von Löwensprung Uffz. Josef Haunstätter	5 5	P Bf		Bf 110 E-1 S9+LN 3447	100%	Shot down on combat mission. Both crewmen returned to unit.	Nokolskoje.
10-12-41	Lt. Karl-Heinz Wildies Uffz. Karl Schnattinger	2 2	P Bf	K K	Me 210 A-1 S9+CK 2266	100%	Crashed on training flight.	Hörsching, near Linz.
14-12-41		2			Bf 110 E-1 3875	35%	Belly-landing due to technical problem.	Orel-West airfield.
16-12-41	Ofw. Leopold Müllauer Uffz. Franz Steuerer	4 4	P Bf	M M	Bf 110 E-2 S9+BM 4524	100%	Did not return from combat mission.	5 Kms. south-west of Srednaja.
16-12-41	Uffz. Erhard Grothe Uffz. Anton Stroka	4 4	P Bf	M M	Bf 110 E-2 S9+MM 4498	100%	Did not return from combat mission.	5 Kms. south-west of Srednaja.
16-12-41	Uffz. Siegfried Jahnke Ofhnr. Manfred Hummel Ogefr. Walther Schneider	5 Ln. Zug 5	P Bf Waffenwart	M M M	Bf 110 C-6 S9+MN 2152	100%	Did not return from combat mission.	5 Kms. south-west of Chomntowo.
16-12-41		I. Gruppe			Me 210 A-1 2273	10%	Forced-landing.	Landsberg-Lech airfield.
16-12-41		I. Gruppe			Me 210 A-1 2277	20%	Forced-landing.	Landsberg-Lech airfield
16-12-41		I. Gruppe			Me 210 A-1 227	20%	Undercarriage failure.	Landsberg-Lech airfield.
23-12-41	Ofw. Ernst Scherer Ofw. Martin Theilmann	6 6	P Bf	M M	Bf 110 E-2 S9+DP 4001	100%	Crash-landed in no-mans land. Crew seen to leave aircraft and head south-west.	Koselsk, south-east of Suchinitschi.
27-12-41	Oblt. Günther Tonne	6	P	W	Bf 110 E-2/ Trop S9+CP 4018		Damaged on combat mission.	Trutky, south of Novosyl.
02-01-42		2			Me 210 A-1 152	45%	Emergency landing due to engine trouble.	Landsberg-Lech airfield.

ZERSTÖRER GESCHWADER 1 LOSS LIST

Date	Name of crew and rank	Staffel	Status	Fate	Aircraft code & W.Nr.	Damage state	Reason for casualty	Place
04-01-42	Lt. Alex Brasse	II. Gruppe	P	K	Bf 110 C-4	75%	Crash-landing	Brjansk airfield.
	Uffz. Hans Kolker	II. Gruppe	Bf	M	3567			
07-01-42	Uffz. Waldemar Keuper	6	P	K	Bf 110 E-1	100%	Non-combat flying accident.	300 metres north-east of
	Ofw. Kurt Huhn	6	O. Wk. Meister	K	S9+BP			Brjansk-south airfield.
	Ogefr. August Bruckmeyer	6	1. Wart	K	3471			
08-01-42		II. Gruppe			Bf 110 C-4	35%	Belly-landing due to airframe damage.	Brjansk airfield.
					2066			
15-01-42	Fw. Gerhard Saretzki	1	P	K	Me 210 A-1	100%	Crashed due to technical problems.	2 Kms. east
	Uffz. Heinz Schulte	1	Bf	K	S9+EH			of Mittelstetten.
					141			
15-01-42		II. Gruppe			Bf 110 E-1	70%	Belly-landing following combat damage.	Orel-West airfield.
					3442			
17-01-42		6			Bf 110 E-1	100%	Crash-landed.	Near Poljudowa.
					3822			
18-01-42		5			Bf 110 E-1	60%	Crash-landed following combat damage	Brjansk.
					3882			
20-01-42		I. Gruppe			Me 210	10%	Belly landing due to technical problem.	Augsburg airfield.
					2278			
24-01-42	Ofw. Günther Schilling	Stab, II.	P	PoW	Bf 110 E-2	100%	Shot down behind Russian lines. Crew seen to get	30 Kms. south-west
	Ofw. Heinz Wiegand	Gruppe	Bf	PoW	S9+TC		away from aircraft.	of Livny.
					4107			
27-01-42		I. Gruppe			Me 210 A-1	20%	Undercarriage failure.	Lechfeld airfield.
					125			
27-01-42		I. Gruppe			Me 210 A-1	15%	Belly landing due to technical and undercarriage failure.	Lechfeld airfield.
					139			
28-01-42		I. Gruppe			Me 210 A-1	35%	Failed take-off.	Lechfeld airfield.
					131			
28-01-42		I. Gruppe			Me 210 A-1	90%	Failed take-off.	Lechfeld airfield.
					143			
31-01-42	Ofw. Otto Rückert	1	P	K	Me 210 A-1	100%	Overturned on landing.	Landsberg-Lech airfield.
					NT+CX			
					080			
31-01-42	Uffz. Hans Tillheim	2	P	K	Me 210 A-1	100%	Overturned on landing.	Landsberg-Lech airfield.
					GT+VH			
					090			
02-02-42		II. Gruppe			Bf 110 C-4		Belly-landing following combat damage.	Brjansk.
					3811			
03-02-42	Hptm. Rolf Kaldrack	Stab, II.	P	K	Bf 110 E-1	100%	S9+TC of Oblt. Ortmann crashed into aircraft.	Basary, 25 Kms. south
	(Gruppenkommandeur)	Gruppe			S9+IC			of Toropyetz.
	Uffz. Martin Enke	Stab, II.	Bf	K	4057			
		Gruppe						
03-02-42	Oblt. Wolfgang Ortmann	Stab, II.	P	K	Bf 110 E-2	100%	Crashed into aircraft of Hptm. Kaldrack.	Basary, 25 Kms. south
		Gruppe						
	Ogefr. Josef Milichowsky	II. Gruppe	Bf	K	S9+TC			of Toropyetz.
					4044			
11-02-42	Oblt. Helmut Lölhöffel	5	P	M	Bf 110 E-2/N	100%	Did not return from combat mission.	4-6 Kms. south-east
	von Löwensprung				S9+HN			of Demidow.
	(Staffelkapitän)				4415			
	Lt. Günther Jochum	5	Bf	M				
14-02-42		Stab, II.			Bf 110 E-1	15%	Damaged while taxi-ing.	Witebsk.
		Gruppe			3916			
14-02-42		6			Bf 110 E-2	20%	Damaged while taxi-ing.	Witebsk.
					4027			
24-02-42	Lt. Karl Kastner	6	P	K	Bf 110 E-2		Killed on combat mission.	10 Kms. west of Ustj.
					S9+BP			
					3539			
24-02-42		II. Gruppe			Bf 110 C-6	40%	Crash-landing due to bad weather	Brjansk.
					2250			
24-02-42		II. Gruppe			Bf 110	40%	Emergency landing following combat damage.	Near Schurawk.
					4042			
27-02-42	Fw. Ludwig Schmidhuber	6	P	K	Bf 110 C-6		Both crewmen killed on combat mission.	South of Moszalsk.
	Ogefr. Robert Kissler	6	Bf	K	S9+SP			
					2249			
28-02-42	Uffz. Hellmuth Rohde	5	P	M	Bf 110 E-2/	100%	Did not return from combat mission.	Schaelanowo.
	Ogefr. Ernst Poths	5	Bf	M	Trop/N			
					S9+FN			
					4495			
28-02-42	Ofw. Gerhard Wittig	5	P	W	Bf 110 E-1/N		Damaged on combat mission.	South-east of
					S9+IN			Suchinitschi.
					4053			
01-03-42	Fw. Georg Schanz	4	P	M	Bf 110 C-4	100%	Did not return from combat mission.	Subowo.
	Gefr. Hermann Müller	4	Bf	M	S9+AM			
					3595			
01-03-42		II. Gruppe			Bf 110 E-1	45%	Crash-landing following combat damage.	Brjansk airfield.
					3822			
03-03-42	Flgr. Otto Steinkraus	1	P	K	Me 210 A-1	100%	Crashed on training flight following problems	7 Kms. west of Tours.
	Gefr. Josef Lugauer	1	Bf	K	S9+IH		with right engine.	
					2273			

Date	Name of crew and rank	Staffel	Status	Fate	Aircraft code & W.Nr.	Damage state	Reason for casualty	Place
03-03-42		1			Me 210 A-1 150	15%	Forced-landing.	Tours airfield.
03-03-42		2			Me 210 A-1 2271	20%	Forced-landing.	Tours airfield.
03-03-42		3			Me 210 A-1 128	25%	Forced-landing.	Tours airfield.
05-03-42		3			Me 210 A-1 139	15%	Belly-landing.	Tours airfield.
07-03-42	Hptm. Walter Poka von Pokafalva (Staffelkapitän and acting-Gruppenkommandeur) Uffz. Gerhard Fricke	4 4	P Bf	K K	Bf 110 E-2 S9+CM 3735	100%	Shot down by Flak on combat mission.	3 Kms. north-east of Staritza.
08-03-42		2			Me 210 A-1 2269	15%	Forced-landing.	Tours airfield.
08-03-42		2			Me 210 A-1 2262	15%	Damaged while taxi-ing.	Tours airfield.
09-03-42		1			Me 210 A-1 2275	20%	Forced-landing.	Tours airfield.
09-03-42		2			Me 210 A-1 2285	20%	Forced-landing.	Tours airfield.
09-03-42	Fw. Hans Helduser Uffz. Hans Biersack	3 3	P Bf	K K	Me 210 A-1 S9+HL 2265	100%	Crashed on training flight, cause not known.	3 Kms. west of Tours.
09-03-42	Lt. Gerhard Schwab Uffz. Karl-Fritz Schröder	3 3	P Bf	W W	Me 210 A-1 S9+IL 2261	65%	Belly-landed due to engine failure.	Tours airfield.
11-04-42		7			Bf 110 D-3 3437	70%	Crash-landing.	Lechfeld airfield.
26-04-42		III. Gruppe			Bf 109 E-7 6472	25%	Crashed on landing.	Lechfeld airfield.
29-04-42		1			Bf 110 F-4 2710	35%	Belly-landing due to engine damage.	Eiling, Ammersee.
30-04-42		III. Gruppe			Bf 109 E-7 3783	40%	Crashed on landing.	Lechfeld airfield.
30-04-42		III. Gruppe			Bf 109 E-7 958	15%	Crashed on landing.	Lechfeld airfield.
01-05-42		III. Gruppe			Bf 109 E-7 1267	10%	Crashed on landing	Lechfeld airfield.
01-05-42		I. Gruppe			Bf 110 D-2 3343	10%	Belly-landing due to technical problems.	Neubiberg.
01-05-42		II. Gruppe			Bf 110 E-2 3779	60%	Damaged while taxi-ing.	Lechfeld airfield.
04-05-42	Fw. Willi Sarnow Gefr. Karl Günther	2 2	P Bf	K K	Bf 110 E-1 S9+DK 3962	100%	Pulled out too late from bombing practise dive.	Ammersee/Obb.
07-05-42	Uffz. Max Skonikowski Gefr. Dietrich Rossdeutscher	5 5	P Bf	K K	Bf 110 E-1 S9+AN 3428	100%	Crashed on non-combat flight.	Lagerlechfeld airfield.
07-05-42	Lt. Friedrich Worscheck	8	P	W	Bf 109 E-7 1507	85%	Crashed on non-combat flight.	Weichertshausen.
08-05-42	Lt. Hans-Georg Schumann Uffz. Winfried Kleck	I. Gruppe	P Bf	K K	Bf 110 F-4 2704	100%	Crashed and burnt-out on non-combat flight.	Neubiberg.
11-05-42	Uffz. Richard Söchtig Uffz. Walter Schwietzer	1 1	P Bf	W K	Bf 110 F-4 2680	85%	Crashed due to technical problem.	Hohenbrunn.
11-05-42		I. Gruppe			Bf 110 F-4 2686	60%	Belly-landing due to servicing fault.	Neubiberg.
12-05-42		8			Bf 109 E-7 2732	30%	Technical problem on non-combat flight.	Near Stuttgart.
13-05-42	Ofhnr. Friedrich Hermes	8	P	K	Bf109 E-7 5199	100%	Part of left wing broke off during steep practise dive and aircraft crashed.	Lagerlechfeld airfield.
14-05-42		II. Gruppe			Bf 109 E-7 4536	20%	Belly-landing due to engine failure.	Near Weilheim.
17-05-42	Uffz. Josef König Gefr. Bruno Trox	6 6	P Bf	K K	Bf 110 E-2 S9+HP 3012	100%	Crashed on non-combat flight.	Neubiberg, south of Munich.
18-05-42		III. Gruppe			Bf 109 E-7 4880	30%	Crashed on take-off.	Lechfeld airfield.
20-05-42		III. Gruppe			Bf 109 E-7 6027	20%	Crashed on take-off.	Prague-Rusin airfield.
21-05-42		7			Bf 109 E-7 818		Technical problems.	Konstantinowka.
21-05-42		8			Bf 109 E-7 707	30%	Belly-landing.	Prague-Rusin airfield.
21-05-42	Lt. Willi Radz	III. Gruppe	P	W	Bf 109 E-7 5357	70%	Overturned on landing.	Saporoshje.
23-05-42		7			Bf 109 E-7 4818	30%	Emergency landing due to running short of fuel.	Kirowograd.
23-05-42	Oblt. Heinrich Dimstbur	9	P		Bf 109 E-7 1789	25%	Reason for damage not known.	Sawinzy.

Date	Name of crew and rank	Staffel	Status	Fate	Aircraft code & W.Nr.	Damage state	Reason for casualty	Place
24-05-42		III. Gruppe			Bf 109 E-7 7669	40%	Crashed on take-off.	Barwenkowo.
25-05-42		I. Gruppe			Bf 110 F-2/ Trop 4534	20%	Airframe damaged.	Neubiberg airfield.
27-05-42	Lt. Walter Grünberg	4	P	K	Bf 110 F-4 S9+FM 2721	100%	Crashed on non-combat flight due to engine failure.	North-east of Ufer, Amersee.
	Uffz. Gottfried Gusenbauer	4	Bf	K				
27-05-42		7			Bf 109 E-7 5627	60%	Emergency landing due to running short of fuel.	Talnoje.
29-05-42	Oblt. Georg Boxhammer (Staffelkapitän)	3	P	K	Bf 110 F-2 S9+LL 4610	100%	Port engine failed after take-off from Krakau airfield. Aircraft crashed.	10 Kms. east of Krakau.
	Uffz. Herbert Knef	3	Bf	K				
	Fw. Georg Pritzel	3	Ground-crew	K				
29-05-42	Uffz. Bruno Baumeister	I. Gruppe	P	W	Bf 110 F-2 26950		Engine failure.	Deutsch-Brod.
	Uffz. Heinz Ludwig	I. Gruppe	Bf	W				
	Uffz. Walter Mieduski	I. Gruppe	Bm	W				
29-05-42		II. Gruppe			Bf 110 F-4 4614	40%	Engine failure.	Krakau.
30-05-42	Ofw Ludwig Mergard	5	P	K	Bf 110 S9+MN 3786	100%	Crashed on non-combat flight.	30 Kms. west of Reichshof.
	Uffz. Waldemar Meyer	5	Bf	K				
	Ogefr. Gerhard Michalowski	5	Ground-crew	K				
31-05-42	Uffz. Werner Zinke	3	P	K	Bf 110 F-2/ Trop S9+JL 4542	100%	Port engine failed after take-off from Lemburg airfield. Aircraft crashed.	Near Lemburg.
	Gefr. Hans Rau	3	Bf	K				
	Uffz. Heinrich Wagner	3	Ground-crew	K				
31-05-42	Fw. Robert Tamm	3	P	K	Bf 110 F-2/ Trop S9+GL 4540	100%	Port engine failed after take-off from Lemburg airfield. Aircraft crashed.	Lemburg airfield.
	Gefr. Franz Wiltsch	3	Bf	K				
	Uffz. Otto Krahn	3	Ground-crew	K				
03-06-42	Oblt. Kurt Seifert	2	P	M	Bf 110 E/U3 S9+SK 4355	100%	Crashed after receiving direct hit from Flak. Gahleitner died in Russian captivity on 26/7/43.	2 Km. north-east of Burluk.
	Uffz. Karl Gahleitner	2	Bf	PoW				
04-06-42		II. Gruppe			Bf 110 E 4449	80%	Undercarriage damage.	Belgorod.
05-06-42		I. Gruppe			Bf 110 D-3 4315	20%	Damaged in bombing attack on airfield.	Belgorod.
05-06-42		III. Gruppe			Bf 109 E-7 4818	80%	Damaged in bombing attack on airfield.	Belgorod.
06-06-42		I. Gruppe			Bf 110 F-2 2702	25%	Airframe damage.	Belgorod.
06-06-42		III. Gruppe			Bf 109 E-7 5946	20%	Belly-landing.	Belgorod.
09-06-42	Oblt. Götz Baumann	6	P	W	Bf 110 E-1 S9+IP 3830	25%	Damaged on combat mission.	3 Kms. south-east of Schejno.
	Gefr. Gustav Haupt	6	Bf	W				
09-06-42		8			Bf 109 E-7 5188	45%	Crashed on take-off.	Belgorod.
10-06-42	Lt. Hans Pilger	Gesch. Stab	P	K	Bf 110 S9+DA 4613F	100%	Did not return from combat mission.	Bodkino, south-south-east of Belgorod.
	Uffz. Helmut Schreiber	Gesch. Stab	Bf	K				
10-06-42	Lt. Bodo von Rabenau	3	P		Bf 110 S9+SL		Force-landed in cornfield.	10 Kms. south-east of Belgorod.
	Uffz. Karl-Fritz Schröder	3	Bf					
10-06-42		3			Bf 110 E-2 4313	10%	Emergency landing due to shortage of fuel.	Near Belgorod.
10-06-42	Lt. Fritz Sax	6	P	M	Bf 110 E/U4 S9+HP 4109	100%	Shot down on combat mission. Sax returned to unit.	North-west of Woltschansk.
	Gefr. Ernst Ries	6	Bf	M				
10-06-42		III. Gruppe Stab			Bf 109 E-7 3547	20%	Hit by Flak.	Belgorod.
11-06-42		1			Bf 110 F-2 2701	10%	Crash-landing.	Lenzewo.
11-06-42	Lt. Kurt Kohler	2	P	K	Bf 110 S9+BK 4089	100%	Crashed after receiving direct hit from Flak.	Lenzewo.
	Uffz. Werner Gebhardt	2	Bf	K				
11-06-42		2			Bf 110 E 3781	10%	Hit by Flak.	Belgorod.
11-06-42		2			Bf 110 E 2381	25%	Hit by Flak.	Belgorod.
11-06-42	Oblt. Albert Heilmayer	6	P	K	Bf 110 E/U-4 S9+KP 4517	100%	Aircraft seen to be shot down by Flak.	Schtschebekino.
	Uffz. Otto Hörger	6	Bf	M				
11-06-42		7			Bf 109 E-7 4943	25%	Damage caused by servicing fault.	
12-06-42		3			Bf 110 E 4292	10%	Crash-landed due to poor ground conditions.	Belgorod.
12-06-42	Ofw. Karl Reich	4	P	K	Bf 110 F-4 S9+BM 2709	100%	Aircraft shot down on approach to airfield.	Belgorod.
	Gefr. Alfred Neu	4	Bf	K				

Date	Name of crew and rank	Staffel	Status	Fate	Aircraft code & W.Nr.	Damage state	Reason for casualty	Place
12-06-42		7			Bf 109 E-7 1193	30%	Crashed on take-off.	Belgorod.
13-06-42		I. Gruppe			Bf 110 E 4427	20%	Crash-landing.	Belgorod.
13-06-42	Fw. Ludwig Betz	5	P		Bf 110 E 4391	30%	Engine failure.	Kasatzkoje.
13-06-42	Uffz. Heinrich Meyer	Stab, III. Gruppe	P	K	Bf109 E-7 S9+DD 6414	100%	Crashed after receiving direct hit from Flak.	Ustinka, near Schebikino.
13-06-42	Uffz. Max Müller	7	P	W	Bf 109 E-7 9642	90%	Damage caused by engine failure. Location not known.	
13-06-42		7			Bf 109 E-7 989		Technical problems.	Belgorod.
19-06-42	Fw. Paul Karwatka Uffz. Wilhelm Leewen	1 1	P Bf	M PoW	Bf 110 F-4 S9+IH 2712	100%	Separated from Staffel in bad weather. Heard to report running short of fuel. Karwatka died later in captivity.	4 Kms. north of Petrowka.
19-06-42	Ofw. Erich Koch Uffz. Hermann Danner	4 4	P Bf	K K	Bf 110 F-4 S9+HM 2720	100%	Crashed following engine failure on combat mission.	Bolchowetz.
19-06-42		8			Bf 109 E-7 811	45%	Crashed on take-off.	Belgorod.
22-06-42	Lt. Gustav Bergmeister Uffz. Lothar Olonczik	3 3	P Bf	M M	Bf 110 S9+GL 3829	100%	Crashed after receiving direct hit from Flak.	30 Kms. west of Kupjansk.
22-06-42	Uffz. Franz Streitberger Gefr. Harald Rudolph	6 6	P Bf	K K	Bf 110 E-2 S9+GP 4111	100 %	Crashed after receiving direct hit from Flak.	6 Kms. south of Isjum.
22-06-42		7			Bf 109 E-7 4915	60%	Crashed on take-off.	Belgorod.
22-06-42		9			Bf 109 E-7 3656	35%	Crashed on take-off.	Belgorod.
22-06-42		9			Bf 109 E-7 4090	20%	Crash-landing.	Belgorod.
22-06-42		III. Gruppe			Bf 109 E-7 6014	30%	Crashed on take-off.	Belgorod.
23-06-42		4			Bf 110 F-4 2717	25%	Damaged on combat mission.	Near Kamyschewacho.
24-06-42		4			Bf 110 E 4086	20%	Crash-landing.	Belgorod.
25-06-42		III. Gruppe			Bf 109 E-7 1338	100%	Burnt-out following the explosion of a fuel tanker on the airfield.	
26-06-42		7			Bf 109 E-7 2747	30%	Crash landing.	Kirowograd.
28-06-42	Uffz. Wilhelm Tögel	3			Bf 110 F-2 43290	55%	Crashed on take-off.	Belgorod.
30-06-42	Ogefr. Gerhard Hermann Ogefr. Günther Neidel	5 5	P Bf	M M	Bf 110 E/U-4 S9+FN 4364	100%	Shot down by Flak on combat mission.	Kruglensky.
30-06-42		5			Bf 110 E 432	50%	Engine failure.	Belgorod.
30-06-42		5			Bf 110 E	10%	Flak damage.	Belgorod.
30-06-42		6			Bf 110 E 3485	25%	Hit by Flak.	Charkow.
30-06-42		8			Bf 109 E-7 707	25%	Damage due to enemy fire.	Belgorod.
30-06-42		8			Bf 109 E-7 7669	10%	Damage due to enemy fire.	
01-07-42	Fw. Helmut Lußky Uffz. Karl-Fritz Schröder	3 3	P Bf		Bf 110 F-2 S9+KL 4096	100%	Shot down by Russian tank, Force-landed 500 metres behind enemy lines. Both crewmen returned to unit.	Babenkoff
01-07-42	Uffz. Werner Ringel	9	P	K	Bf109 E-7 989	100%	Overturned on take-off.	Welikaja-Wischnewaja.
02-07-42	Uffz. Ludwig Kastner Uffz. Gerhard Losse	6 6	P Bf	M M	Bf 110 E-2/U4 S9+SP 3976	100%	Shot down by Flak during low-level attack. Both crewmen killed by Russian partisans.	3 Kms. east of Priwoljno.
02-07-42	Ogefr. Waldemar Müller	8	P	W	Bf 109 E-7 1254	50%	Hit by Flak.	Korotscha.
03-07-42		III. Gruppe			Bf 109 E-7 694	50%	Overturned on landing.	Woroschilow.
04-07-42	Oblt. Rudolf Thomas Uffz. Heinrich Theissen	2 2	P Bf	 W	Bf 110 E S9+MK 4099		Aircraft crash-landed following combat with Russian fighters.	Bolsche-Iwanowka.
04-07-42	Uffz. Heinz Melchart Uffz. Hans Ziesche	5 5	P Bf		Bf 110 E 3782	50%	Crash-landing.	Near Duidjanny.
04-07-42	Ofw. Ernst Melzer	6	P		Bf 110 E S9+BP 4007	50%	Hit by Flak.	Nikolajewka.
07-07-42		5			Bf 110 E 4079	50%	Damaged by enemy fire.	Kolokonoka airfield.

Date	Name of crew and rank	Staffel	Status	Fate	Aircraft code & W.Nr.	Damage state	Reason for casualty	Place
07-07-42		9			Bf 109 E-7 6310	25%	Emergency landing due to shortage of fuel.	Near Kupjansk.
08-07-42		5			Bf 110 E-3 4090	20%	Airframe damaged while taxi-ing.	Konstantinowka airfield.
09-07-42	Uffz. Willi Führe	2	Bf	W	Bf 110 S9+DK 4040		Damaged in combat with Russian fighters.	Messarosch, near Lissitschansk.
09-07-42	Uffz. Wilhelm Tögel	3	P	W	Bf 110 S9+HL 4541		Damaged in combat with Russian fighters.	20 Kms. west of Salawiansk.
09-07-42		6			Bf 110 E-3 4455	20%	Airframe damaged on take-off.	Konstantinowka airfield.
09-07-42		6			Bf 110 E-1 4022	50%	Damage due to enemy action.	Near Belokarowka.
09-07-42	Uffz. Emil Pfeiffer	6	P		Bf 110	60%	Damage due to enemy fighter action.	Konstantinowka.
10-07-42		7			Bf 109 E-7 3547	20%	Hit by Flak.	Belgorod.
13-07-42	Lt. Joachim Hacker Uffz. Kurt Steenbock	4 4	P Bf	M K	Bf 110 F-4 S9+EM 2722	100%	Shot down on combat mission. Pilot returned to unit.	Krassnaja-Telowka.
13-07-42		4			Bf 110 F-4 2724	70%	Belly-landing following combat with fighters.	Konstantinowka airfield.
13-07-42		6			Bf 110 E 4345	35%	Damaged while taxi-ing.	Konstantinowka airfield.
13-07-42	Lt. Heinz Friedmann	7	P	W	Bf 109 E-7 1090	60%	Reason for damage not known.	Konstantinowka.
13-07-42	Uffz. Manfred Kuhn	8	P	M	Bf109 E-7 S9+CS 3572	100%	Did not return from combat mission.	15 Kms. north-north-east of Woroschilowgrad.
13-07-42	Ofw. Wilhelm Dibowski Uffz. Kurt Meier	5 5	P Bf		Bf 110 S9+EN 4054	50%	Left engine damaged by Flak while attacking Russian tanks. Force-landed.	Near Woroschilowgrad.
14-07-42		9			Bf 109 E-7 2047	60%	Engine failure.	Krinitschnaja.
15-07-42		7			Bf 109 E-7 4943	30%	Emergency landing.	Semyj.
16-07-42	Uffz. Peter Varga	II. Gruppe	Bm		Caudron C445 437	80%	Crashed on take-off.	Konstantinowka airfield.
17-07-42	Fw. Hugo Steiger Uffz. Schwarz	2 2	P Bf		Bf 110 S9+HK 3952	100%	Direct hit from Flak. Crew baled out behind German lines unhurt.	North of Kamensk.
18-07-42		8			Bf 109 E-7 1546	30%	Airframe damaged on landing.	Kuteinikowo.
19-07-42		3			Bf 110 E-2 8545	20%	Emergency landing due to technical problems.	
20-07-42	Uffz. Gustav Melzheimer Gefr. Werner Schulz	3 3	P Bf	K W	Bf 110 E-1 S9+TL 3835	70%	Crashed on take-off on non-combat flight.	Tschernobay.
20-07-42		5			Bf 110 E-2 4400	100%	Hit by Flak.	Sulinskaja.
21-07-42	Oblt. Otto Christian Ogefr. Eduard Peitz	6 6	P Bf	M M	Bf 110 E 3694	50%	Forced down due to enemy action. Oblt. Christian later returned to unit.	Near Marjewka.
21-07-42	Uffz. Werner Voss	7	P		Bf 109 E-7 S9+FR 3439	30%	Emergency landing.	Karschinow-Iwanosk.
21-07-42	Lt. Hugo Sander	8	P	K	Bf109 E-7 890		Pilot killed on combat mission.	Kuteinikowo.
22-07-42	Hptm. Dominikus Kneidl (Staffelkapitän)	8	P	M	Bf109 E-7 S9+LS 4212	100%	Did not return from combat mission.	North-east of Rostow.
22-07-42	Uffz. Emil Hauk	8	P	M	Bf109 E-7 S9+AS 7659	100%	Did not return from combat mission.	North-east of Rostow.
22-07-42		8			Bf 109 E-7 5935	60%	Crashed on take-off.	Kuteinikowo.
23-07-42		II. Gruppe			Bf 110 2719	25%	Damage due to enemy action.	Near Salan-Saly.
25-07-42		1			Bf 110 F-2 2714	10%	Crash-landing.	Nowo-Lakademinowka.
25-07-42		6			Bf 110 E 4466		Hit by Flak.	Near Micailowkow.
26-07-42	Oblt. Kurt Scheffel (Staffelkapitän) Fw. Albert Schieder	1 1	P Bf	W	Bf 110 F-2 S9+CH 2688		Pilot wounded on combat mission.	
26-07-42		2			Bf 110 F-2 4598	10%	Airframe damage.	Nowo-Lakademinowka.
27-07-42		1			Bf 110 F 4305	10%	Hit by Flak.	Near Rostow.
27-07-42		4			Bf 110 F-4 4628	40%	Hit by Flak.	Bataisk.

Date	Name of crew and rank	Staffel	Status	Fate	Aircraft code & W.Nr.	Damage state	Reason for casualty	Place
01-08-42		1			Bf 110 F-4 4089	50%	Emergency landing due to engine failure.	
01-08-42	Lt. Oswald Ries Gefr. Günther Dorsch	2	P Bf		Bf 110 3991	100%	Shot down by Flak. Crew returned to unit.	Near Popo.
01-08-42	Gefr. Franz Ernst	4		M	Bf 110 3916	60%	Belly-landed after receiving hits.	Near Seschtschinskaja.
01-08-42		6			Bf 110 D-3 4339	50%	Damaged in Russian air attack on airfield.	Dimitrijewkaya airfield.
03-08-42		III. Gruppe			Bf 109 E-7 6122	35%	Crash-landing.	Taganrog airfield.
04-08-42	Uffz. Karl Rottler	4	Bf	K	Bf 110		Bordfunker killed on combat mission.	Rostow.
04-08-42		5			Bf 110 4526	70%	Combat damage from fighters.	Near Kranpotki.
04-08-42		6			Bf 110 E-2 3846	50%	Damaged in Russian air attack on airfield.	Dimitrijewkaya airfield.
04-08-42		6			Bf 110 3739	50%	Damaged in Russian air attack on airfield.	Dimitrijewkaya airfield.
05-08-42	Fw. Ludwig Betz Uffz. Andreas Schmalzl	5 5	P Bf	K K	Bf 110 C-4/ U-3 S9+TN 2130	100%	Shot down by Russian Flak on combat mission.	3 Kms. south-east of Armawir.
08-08-42	Ofw. Herbert Braune Uffz. Herbert Schmalisch	6 6	P Bf	K K	Bf 110 D-3/ U-4 S9+OP 4233	100%	Shot down in low level attack.	13 Kms. south-west of Krugannaja.
08-08-42		II. Gruppe			Bf 109 F-4 4633	35%	Belly-landing due to combat damage.	Alejwskiy.
09-08-42	Fw. Lothar Uhlig Uffz. Hans Bumbek	6 6	P Bf		Bf 110 E S9+UP 3425		Shot down on combat mission. Crew returned to unit after being posted missing.	Near Oglagskaja.
10-08-42	Ogefr. Oskar Stellmacher	Stab, II. Gruppe	Bf	W	Bf 110 F-4 4608	100%	Shot down on combat mission.	Kuschorskaja.
10-08-42	Oblt. Ernst Haberland Uffz. Heinz Danigel	Erpr. St. 210 Erpr. St. 210	P Bf	M M	Me 210 A-1 GF+CB 2322	100%		
11-08-42	Oblt. Kurt Schröder Uffz. Karl-Günther Lämmel	1 1	P Bf	K K	Bf 110 E-2 S9+OH 2649	100%	Shot down by Russian Lagg-3. Crashed into the sea.	
11-08-42	Lt. Otto Kempf Uffz. Heinz Bothe (1. Wart)	1 1	P Bf	M M	Bf 110 F-2 S9+KH 2713	100%	Missing after combat with Russian Rata fighter.	7-10 Kms. east of Tenrjuk.
12-08-42		I. Gruppe			Bf 110 3908	100%	Destroyed by own bomb exploding.	Bagerowo airfield.
13-08-42		I. Gruppe			Bf 110 E-2 4410	15%	Fuselage damaged on landing.	Bagerowo airfield.
14-08-42	Lt. Heinz Brandes	5	P		Bf 110 3823	90%	Force-landed following hit from Flak.	Armawir.
15-08-42		Gesch. Stab			Bf 110 F-4 4606	40%	Belly-landed following hit from Flak.	Twerskaja.
17-08-42		II. Gruppe			Bf 110 F-4 4604	70%	Belly-landing following damage on combat mission.	Lijskaja.
17-08-42		III. Gruppe			Bf 109 E-7 5962	60%	Collided with Ju 52 on landing.	Proskurow airfield.
18-08-42		4			Bf 110 F-4 4611	40%	Damaged by enemy action on combat mission.	Near Micailowskaja.
18-08-42	Lt. Rudolf Schummer Uffz. Karl Weninger	6 6	P Bf	 K	Bf 110 C S9+RP 2109	100%	Aircraft hit by Flak. Weninger baled out but parachute did not fully open.	6 Kms. west of Krymskaja.
18-08-42		6			Bf 110 E-2 S9+NP 3009	10%	Damage due to enemy action.	Abinskaja.
19-08-42					Bf 110 4027	40%	Engine damaged by enemy action.	Krasnodar.
21-08-42	Fw. Adolf Gross Uffz. Friedrich Frese	1 1	P Bf	K K	Bf 110 E-1 S9+SH 4064	100%	Russian munitions dump exploded during low-level attack and brought down aircraft.	3 Kms. south-east of Schuleaujakow.
22-08-42		Stab, III. Gruppe			Bf 109 E-4 2051	10%	Crashed on take-off.	Schleißheim airfield.
22-08-42		III. Gruppe			Bf 109 E-1 3339	10%	Belly-landing due to servicing fault.	Schleißheim airfield.
22-08-42		III. Gruppe			Bf 109 E-4 4730	10%	Crash-landed due to bad ground conditions.	Schleißheim airfield.
23-08-42		2			Bf 110 E 3475	100%	Engine failure. Crew unhurt,	
23-08-42		III. Gruppe			Bf 109 E-7 948	25%	Technical problem	Bad Vöslau
24-08-42	Lt. Franz Busch Gefr. Heinz Schaller	5 5	P Bf		Bf 110 E 3460	80%	Damaged by enemy fire.	Andrejedmitrijwka.
25-08-42	Lt. Heinrich Dankworth	Stab, I. Gruppe	P	K	Bf 110 F-2 S9+AB	100%	Shot down by Russian Flak on combat mission.	30 Kms. west-north-west of Stalingrad.

Date	Name of crew and rank	Staffel	Status	Fate	Aircraft code & W.Nr.	Damage state	Reason for casualty	Place
	Uffz. Georg Reuther Oblt. Gerhard Hoffmann	1 2 Ln-Zug	Bf Bs	K K	2706			
26-08-42					Bf 110 D-3 3377	70%	Engine failure.	
28-08-42		1			Bf 110 D 4230	30%	Belly-landing due to engine failure.	
28-08-42		I. Gruppe			Bf 110 D 1391	15%	Damaged in enemy bombing attack on airfield.	Armawir airfield.
28-08-42		3			Bf 110 C 2189	10%	Damaged in enemy bombing attack on airfield.	Plowir airfield.
28-08-42		6			Bf 110 E 4479	90%	Engine failure due to enemy hits.	Chadyahenskaja.
29-08-42		1			Bf 110 S9+BH		Emergency landing following combat.	Near Plewistyi.
31-08-42	Uffz. Josef Müller	2			Bf 110 E 3942	70%	Engine damage.	Frohlof airfield.
31-08-42	Uffz. Hans Sennholz	7	P	PoW	Bf109 E-7 S9+DR 4964		Shot down on combat mission by ground fire.	Near El Alamein.
31-08-42		III. Gruppe			Bf 109 E 3551	80%	Crash-landing.	
01-09-42		5			Bf 110 C 2066	35%	Hit by Flak,	Noworossisk.
01-09-42	Major Roland Borth	Stab, III. Gruppe	P	K	Bf109 E-7 S9+AD 6305	100%	Shot down by 15 enemy fighters. Died in hospital on 09-09-42	East of El Alamein.
02-09-42	Uffz. Richard Heinrich Uffz. Kurt Gerschütz	2 2	P Bf	K K	Bf 110 S9+GK 4092	100%	Russian fighter put one engine out of action. Aircraft crashed.	West of Stalingrad.
02-09-42	Uffz. Schreiber Stfw. Barthlau	3 3	P Bf	 W	Bf 110 S9+SL 3930	100%	Emergency landing following hits from enemy fighter.	5 Kms. north-north-east of Rossoschka.
02-09-42	Lt. Joachim Hacker Uffz. Alfred Steinweg	4 4	P Bf	M M	Bf 110 D S9+EM 4281	100%	Did not return from combat mission.	South-west of Dubowka, near Stalingrad.
02-09-42	Uffz. Johannes Rauhut	8	P	K	Bf109 E-7 4140	100%	Crashed on take-off, colliding with a crash-landed Bf 110.	Bir el Abd airfield.
03-09-42		Stab, I. Gruppe			Bf 110 S9+BB		Emergency landing following hits from ground fire.	2 Kms. north-north-east of Malyi.
03-09-42		1			Bf 110 F-2 2718	35%	Hit by Flak.	
03-09-42		2			Bf 110 E-1 4112	35%	Engine failure.	
04-09-42		1			Bf 110 D S9+OH 4240		Direct hit from Flak.	4 1/2 Kms. south-east of Solotoj Rog.
04-09-42	Lt. Karl-Heinz Heinelt Uffz. Otto Ehmann	5 5	P Bf	K W	Bf 110 D-3 S9+KN 4346		Pilot killed on combat mission.	8 Kms. north of Ssewerskaja.
05-09-42		III. Gruppe			Bf 109 E 1587		Belly-landing.	Turbiya.
06-09-42	Oblt. Karl-Heinz Dzianowski	6	P	W	Bf 110 E-1 S9+IP 3830	40%	Belly-landed following damage to engine caused by enemy action.	Kerenskaja.
07-09-42		2			Bf 110 E S9+KK 3445	15%	Explosion caused by engine backfiring.	Frohlof airfield.
07-09-42		5			Bf 110 E 3881	50%	Damaged by enemy fire.	Jelisawetinskaja airfield.
08-09-42		6			Bf 110 E 3434	60%	Engine failure following hits in combat.	Near Krimskaja.
09-09-42	Uffz. Klaus Schulze	2	Bf	M	Bf 110		Missing following combat. Later returned to unit.	
10-09-42		3			Bf 110 D 3656	25%	Damaged by Flak.	Frohlof.
10-09-42	Uffz. Rudolf Edelbauer	4	P	K	Bf 110		Pilot killed on combat mission.	Near Kotluban.
12-09-42		III. Gruppe			Bf 109 F-4/ Trop 6269	70%	Crashed on take-off.	Bir el Abd airfield.
13-09-42	Uffz. Hans Jurgen Narten	4	Bf	W	Bf 110		Bordfunker wounded on combat mission.	Kotluban, near Stalingrad.
14-09-42	Ofw. WIlli Lukas	2	Bf	K	Bf 110 E S9+KK 3996	80%	Collided with Bf 110 E, W.Nr.3958, while landing.	Frohlof airfield.
14-09-42		2			Bf 110 3958	60%	Collided with Bf 110 E, S9+KK, W.Nr.3996, while landing.	Frohlof airfield.
14-09-42		III. Gruppe			Bf 109 E 1237	70%	Crashed on take-off.	Bir el Abd airfield.
15-09-42		1			Bf 110 S9+FH 2699	100%	Emergency landing.	Near Gumrak, south-west of Stalingrad.

Date	Name of crew and rank	Staffel	Status	Fate	Aircraft code & W.Nr.	Damage state	Reason for casualty	Place
15-09-42		5			Bf 110 E 4371	60%	Damage due to enemy fire.	Naienokaoja.
16-09-42		6			Bf 110 D 4329	20%	Hit by enemy fighter.	
17-09-42	Lt. Heinz Brandes	5	P	W	Bf 110 S9+PN 3905	80%	Pilot wounded on combat mission.	Ischerskaja.
17-09-42	Uffz. Gottfried Seifert Uffz. Alfred Brandt	5 5	P Bf	M M	Bf 110 E-2 S9+UN 2542	100%	Rammed by Russian fighter on combat mission.	15 Kms. east of Ischerskaja.
17-09-42		6			Bf 110 E 3771	35%	Damaged while taxi-ing.	Gonschtakowa airfield.
17-09-42	Uffz. Max Müller	7	P	M	Bf109 E-7 S9+CR 4835	100%	Crashed on combat mission.	50 Kms. south of El Hamman.
18-09-42	Oblt. Robert Gebhardt (Staffelkapitän) Fw. Karl-Heinz Menzel	3 3	P Bf	K K	Bf 110 E S9+FL 4344	100%	Aircraft hit by ground fire - crashed returning from mission.	1Km. north-east of Jelampieskij.
19-09-42	Oblt. Theo Kehl (Staffelkapitän) Uffz. Alfred Daniger	1 1	P Bf	M M	Bf 110 F S9+AH 4541	100%	Shot down by Russian fighters.	South of Kotluban railway station.
19-09-42	Uffz. Richard Söchtig Uffz. Heinrich Diemer	1 1	P Bf	M M	Bf 110 D S9+PH 3713	100%	Shot down by Russian fighters.	South of Kotluban railway station.
19-09-42		4			Bf 110 2681	50%	Damaged by fighters.	
20-09-42	Lt. Hans Walter	2	P	K	Bf 110 E S9+FK 4490	100%	Crashed after combat with Russian fighters. Bordfunker returned to unit.	5 Kms. north-west of Bol Rossoschka.
22-09-42		I. Gruppe			Bf 110 F-4 4640	30%	Emergency landing due to servicing fault.	Breslau-Gandau airfield.
24-09-42		4			Bf 110 0152	60%	Damage to undercarriage.	Wolowo-Krasnodar.
25-09-42		II. Gruppe			Bf 110 E 4481	90%	Engine failure following enemy hits.	Zarkoqaj.
27-09-42		II. Gruppe			Bf 110 C	60%	Crashed on take-off.	Krasnodar airfield.
28-09-42		I. Gruppe			Bf 110 C 1400	45%	Crash-landing.	
29-09-42		6			Bf 110 C 3650	50%	Hit during enemy attack on airfield.	Krasnodar airfield.
30-09-42		3			Bf 110 E 3422	80%	Collided with Kl. 35 of Stab, St.G.2 on landing.	Obliwskaja.
01-10-42	Uffz. Heinz Trapp	5	Bf	W	Bf 110 E-2/U-4 S9+FN 3758	10%	Bordfunker wounded on combat mission.	Kurapskaja.
02-10-42	Lt. Walter Burger	8	P	K	Bf109 E-7 775	100%	Shot down by enemy fighter.	40 Kms. south-west of El Alamein.
02-10-42	Lt. Norbert Schmidt	8	P	W	Bf109 E-7 S9+IS 6431	100%	Shot down by enemy fighter.	Near El Alamein.
02-10-42	Uffz. Karl Scheiter	III. Gruppe	P	W	Bf 109 E 6339	80%	Belly-landing due to engine failure.	Bir el Abd airfield.
03-10-42	Uffz. Karl-Heinz Wolf Uffz. Walter Kuhlmann	4 4	P Bf	M M	Bf 110 C-4 S9+CM 3540	100%	Did not return from combat mission.	Orlowka, north-north-west of Stalingrad.
04-10-42		II. Gruppe			Bf 110 E 2723	15%	Airframe damaged while taxi-ing.	Krasnodar airfield.
05-10-42	Lt. Oswald Ries Uffz. Karl Weber	4 4	P Bf		Bf 110 D S9+JK 3807	35%	Damaged by Flak.	
07-10-42		4			Bf 110 F 4629	35%	Damage to undercarriage on take-off.	Frohlof airfield.
07-10-42		II. Gruppe			Bf 110 F 2554	15%	Damaged in combat.	Near Tuapse.
08-10-42	Oblt. Gerhard Walther	5	P	W	Bf 110 E-1 S9+JN 4053		Pilot wounded on combat mission.	South of Fronarberg.
08-10-42	Lt. Werner Damm Uffz. August Krieger	5 5	P Bf	M M	Bf 110 E-2 S9+TN 4356	100%	Hit by Flak. Did not return from combat mission.	20 Kms. south of Gorjatsch-Kljutsch.
09-10-42		III. Gruppe			Bf 109 E 6222	35%	Damaged in enemy attack on airfield.	Bir el Abd airfield.
11-10-42		III. Gruppe			Bf 109 E 1406	100%	Emergency landing due to hits from Flak.	West of Salzsee.
13-10-42		III. Gruppe			Bf 109 E 5809	75%	Crashed on landing.	Bir el Abd airfield.
15-10-42		III. Gruppe			Me 210 A-1 172	20%	Crashed on take-off.	Wiener-Neustadt airfield.
20-10-42		III. Gruppe			Bf 109 E 4014	100%	Emergency landing following hits from Flak.	

Date	Name of crew and rank	Staffel	Status	Fate	Aircraft code & W.Nr.	Damage state	Reason for casualty	Place
21-10-42	Ofw. Hermann Ross Uffz. Horst Tullney	4 4	P P	M M	Bf 110 E-2 S9+VM 3776	100%	Seen to be hit in left engine. Did not return from combat mission.	South-west of Schaumjan.
23-10-42	Ofw. Kurt Krämer Uffz. Michael Klassen	1 1	P Bf	M M	Bf 110 D-3 S9+LH 3683	100%	Missing behind Russian lines.	Schirinka-Ssadowoje.
23-10-42	Lt. Franz Apel Ogefr. Werner Greiner	2 2	P Bf	K K	Bf 110 D-1 S9+SK 2282	100%	Shot down in flames by Russian Flak.	Georgiewskoje.
23-10-42	Uffz. Adolf Blaschke Gefr. Rudolf Fritz	8 8	P Bf	K K	Me 210 A-1 VC+SW 159	100%	Crashed on non-combat flight.	Wiener-Neustadt airfield.
23-10-42		III. Gruppe			Bf 109 E 1458		Emergency landing due to enemy fire.	
24-10-42	Oblt. Rolf Unger	7	P	M	Bf 109 E 2682	100%	Shot down by Flak over enemy territory.	3 Kms. north of Himeimat.
24-10-42		III. Gruppe			Bf 109 E 3339	80%	Crashed on landing.	Bir el Abd airfield.
26-10-42	Uffz. Josef Gebhart	II. Gruppe	Bf	W			Wounded on combat mission.	Near Gisel.
30-10-42		III. Gruppe			Me 210 A-1 034	100%	Engine failure on take-off.	Iraklion airfield.
02-11-42	Fw. Herbert Grünther Uffz. Herbert Grünacher Ogefr. Ernst Bedorf	5 5 5	P Bf 1. Wart	K K K	Bf 110 D-3 S9+EN 4305	100%	Crashed on non-combat flight.	5 Kms. east of Krasnodar airfield.
02-11-42		III. Gruppe			Me 210 197	20%	Crash landing due to engine damage.	Iraklion airfield.
03-11-42	Uffz. Erich Richter	3	P		Bf 110 E 4292	60%	Hit by Flak.	Krasnodar.
05-11-42	Oblt. Hermann Smend	4	P	W	Bf 110 C-4 S9+AM 3091		Pilot wounded on combat mission.	Arechonka.
05-11-42	Uffz. Kurt Steiner	4	Bf	W	Bf 110 C-4 S9+HM 3815		Bordfunker wounded on combat mission.	Gisel.
05-11-42	Hptm. Harald Zimmermann Uffz. Stumpf	III. Gruppe III. Gruppe	P Bf	W W	Me 210 A 177	100%	Crashed following engine damage.	Araxes.
08-11-42		III. Gruppe			Me 210 A-1 2N+AT 039	25%	Belly landing.	Castelli airfield.
10-11-42	Hptm. August Bier Uffz. Hermann Bitrich	2 2	P Bf		Bf 110 E S9+IK 3436	100%	Emergency landing due to engine damage.	Srowdnje.
11-11-42	Fw. Michelmann	I. Gruppe			Bf 110 D-3 3706	35%	Belly-landing due to engine failure.	Groß-Marschwitz.
12-11-42		III. Gruppe			Me 210 A 188	20%	Technical failure.	Trapani.
13-11-42	Oblt. Philipp Bender Uffz. Engelbert Schick	8 8	P Bf	PoW M	Me 210 A 2N+CR 2293	100%	Missing following combat with two Spitfires.	Bougie.
13-11-42		III. Gruppe			Me 210 A 163	100%	Emergency landing due to enemy fire. Aircraft destroyed by own troops.	
13-11-42	Uffz. Hans Krüger Uffz. Rudolf Faißt	11 11	P Bf	M M	Me 210 A 3E+NQ 075	100%	Did not return from combat mission.	30 Kms. east of Algiers.
14-11-42	Uffz. Erwin Seeliger Gefr. Kurt Enke Uffz. Johann List *(9./ZG 1 crew flying a 9./ZG 26 Bf 110)*	9 9	P Bf	M M	Bf 110 E 3U+NT 4412	100%	Missing on non-combat mission.	Between Castelli and Araxos.
16-11-42	Lt. Werner Niclaus Uffz. Eric Staal	10 10	P Bf	K K	Bf 110 F 5065	100%	Crashed, reason not known.	Near Malacky.
18-11-42	Hptm. Kurt Bruegmann Ofw. Kurt Derday	Gesch. Stab Gesch. Stab	P Bf	M M	Bf 110 F S9+BA 4612	100%	Did not return from combat mission.	Tuapse.
18-11-42	Oblt. Heinz Redlich (Staffelkapitän) Fw. Friedrich Hamburger	8 8	P Bf	M M	Me 210 A-1 2N+GS 036	100%	Shot down by Flak from ship on combat mission.	North-east of Appollonia.
18-11-42	Uffz. Hans Zeisch *(8th Staffel crew flying a 9th Staffel Bf 110)*	8	Bf	W	Me 210 2N+DT 057		Bordfunker wounded on combat mission.	North-east of Appollonia.
23-11-42	Fw. Harry Dorst Uffz. Hans Stoltenberg	1 1	P Bf	M M	Bf 110 E S9+TH 4008	100%	Did not return from combat mission.	Stalingrad area.
25-11-42	Lt. Erhard Witzke Uffz. Günther Schmidt *(1st Staffel crew flying a 2nd Staffel Bf 110)*	1 1	P Bf	M M	Bf 110 D-3 S9+KK 2247	100%	Shot down by Flak.	9 Kms. south-west of Donschtschinska.
25-11-42	Lt. Walter Hanke Gefr. Heinrich Auer	7 7	P Bf	K K	Me 210 A-1 2N+DR 073	100%	Received direct hit from Flak on combat mission.	West of Medjez el Bab.
25-11-42		9			Me 210 A-1 068	60%	Damaged due to technical failure.	Trapani.

Date	Name of crew and rank	Staffel	Status	Fate	Aircraft code & W.Nr.	Damage state	Reason for casualty	Place
25-11-42		9			Me 210 A-1	80%	Force-landed following combat.	Near Tunis.
					051			
25-11-42		11			Me 210 A-1	50%	Force-landed following combat.	Near Tunis.
					060			
25-11-42		11			Me 210 A-1	30%	Damaged due to enemy action.	Trapani.
					186			
26-11-42	Uffz. Alfred Koch	2	P	K	Bf 110 E	100%	Crashed on works flight.	3 Kms. west
	Uffz. Johann Dworazyk	2	Bf	K	S9+KK			of Wifljanzew.
	Prüfmeister Friedrich Frese	Stabs Kp.		K	3445			
26-11-42	Hptm. Kurt Loos	7	P	K	Me 210 A-1	100%	Shot down in combat with RAF fighters.	South-west of Medjez
	(Staffelkapitän)				2N+BR			el Bab.
	Ofw. Heinz Schrodt	7	Bf	PoW	155			
27-11-42		7			Me 210	30%	Damaged on landing	
					038			
28-11-42		I. Gruppe			Bf 110 E	15%	Crashed on take-off.	Tazinskaja.
					2377			
28-11-42		II. Gruppe			Bf 110 F	40%	Hit by Flak.	
					5102			
28-11-42		11			Me 210	30%	Damaged on landing.	Trapani.
					164			
29-11-42		Gesch. Stab			Bf 110 F	30%	Emergency landing in bad weather.	Kropotkin airfield.
					5172			
29-11-42		I. Gruppe			Bf 110 E	30%	Engine damage.	Tazinskaja.
					4534			
29-11-42	Hptm. Friedrich Plank	11	P	M	Me 210 A-1	100%	Did not return from combat mission.	20 Kms. south of Tunis.
	(Staffelkapitän)				2N+MV			
	Fw. Heinz Pastoors	11	Bf	M	031			
29-11-42	Fw. Heinrich Brumhuber	12	P	K	Fw 58	100%	Crashed due to technical problems.	Klein-Würben,
	Fw. Emil Dödtke	12	(P)	K				
	Uffz. Günther Staar	12	Bf	K	3314			
02-12-42	Uffz. Helmut Leicht	6		K	Bf 110 E-2		Killed on non-combat flight.	20 Kms. north-west
	(6th Staffel crew in 5th Staffel machine)				S9+CN			of Kertsch.
					4002			
02-12-42	Uffz. Gustav Naumann	9	Bf	W	Me 210 A-1		Bordfunker wounded on combat mission.	Tebourba.
					2N+DT			
					057			
03-12-42		III. Gruppe			Me 210 A-1	100%	Loss occurred due to enemy fire.	Tunis
					065			
04-12-42	Lt. Alwin Meyer	9	P	W	Me 210 A-1	100%	Crew wounded on combat mission. Aircraft a write-off.	50 Kms. east of Faid.
	Uffz. Karl Morgenröther	9	Bf	W	2N+AT			
					071			
04-12-42	Fl. Stabsing. Pfister	11	P	M	Me 210 A-1	100%	Pilot missing, Bordfunker wounded on combat mission.	60 Kms. south
	Ogefr. Günther Weber	11	Bf	W	2N+QV			of Kairun.
					192			
04-12-42		III. Gruppe			Me 210 A-1	100%	Destroyed in bombing attack on airfield.	Tunis.
					099			
05-12-42		9			Me 210 A-1	35%	Aircraft damaged in bombing attack.	Biserta.
					2N+DT			
					057			
05-12-42		III. Gruppe			Me 210 A-1	100%	Hit by AA fire. Aircraft written off. Crew unhurt.	Near Reyville.
					812			
06-12-42	Lt. Fritz Malt	8	P	M	Me 210 A-1	100%	Did not return from combat mission.	100 Kms. west of Sfax.
	Uffz. Fritz Meiser	8	Bf	M	2N+BR			
	(8th Staffel crew in 7th Staffel machine)				246			
07-12-42	Lt. Harro Douglas	3	P	K	Bf 110	100%	Shot down by Flak on combat mission.	Ssurowikuno.
	Fw. Herbert Engel	3	Bf	K	S9+GL			
					4221			
07-12-42	Uffz. Heinz Kossmann	3	Bf	W			Hit by ground fire.	
07-12-42		III. Gruppe			Me 210 A-1	30%	Crashed on take-off.	Trapani.
					174			
08-12-42		3			Bf 110 E	80%	Damaged in bombing attack.	Tazinskaja.
					1991			
10-12-42		III. Gruppe			Me 210 A-1	90%	Ground-looped during landing.	Catania.
					189			
11-12-42		III. Gruppe			Me 210 A-1	100%	Reason for loss not known. Crew unhurt.	Trapani.
					053			
16-12-42	Uffz. Gerhard Motl	4	P	M	Bf 110 E-2	100%	Did not return from combat mission.	Bagajewskaja/Don.
	Uffz. Karl Schildbach	4	Bf	M	S9+RM			
					2382			
16-12-42		4			Bf 110 F	100%	Enemy hits.	
					5067			
16-12-42	Fw. Heinz Döscher	4	P		Bf 110 E	100%		
	Uffz. Eduard Janik	4	Bf		S9+IM			
					3527			
16-12-42	Lt. Gottfried Kayl	5	P		Bf 110 E	100%		
	Uffz. Hans Fuchs	5	Bf		S9+HN			
					3845			
17-12-42	Uffz. Kurt Laaser	3	P	M	Bf 110 E	100%	Did not return from combat mission.	Werelnekermojarsky.
	Uffz. Artur Scharff	3	Bf	M	S9+KL			
					4368			

Date	Name of crew and rank	Staffel	Status	Fate	Aircraft code & W.Nr.	Damage state	Reason for casualty	Place
17-12-42	Fw. Alois Sonntag	5	P	W	Bf 110 C-7		Both crewmen wounded on combat mission.	3 Kms. south
	Uffz. Christian Messner	5	Bf	W	S9+LP			of Ssulazki.
	(5th Staffel crew in a 6th Staffel machine)				3100			
17-12-42	Uffz. Hans-Georg Schmidtal	5	P	W	Bf 110 E-2		Wounded on combat mission.	Werchnij-Kumskij.
	Gefr. Helmut-Karl Hils	5	Bf	W	S9+MN			
					3768			
18-12-42	Lt. Oswald Reis	2	P	M	Bf 110 C	100%	Did not return following combat with Russian fighters.	West of Stalingrad.
	Uffz. Gert Adelhöfer	2	Bf	M	S9+RK			
					2122			
18-12-42	Uffz. Hans Kanzian	3	P	K	Bf 110 E	100%	Crashed on non-combat flight.	Babowka.
	Uffz. Erich Richter	3	(P)	K	S9+BL			
	Ofw. Helmut Lindau	3	Bf	K	2428			
18-12-42	Fw. Heinrich Cassau	3	P	W	Bf 110	70%	Wounded on combat mission following hit from Flak.	1Km. north of
	Uffz. Hans Steckmann	3	Bf	W	S9+NL			Millerowo airfield.
					5777			
18-12-42		III. Gruppe			Me 210 A-1	20%	Ground-looped during landing.	Trapani.
					190			
19-12-42	Lt. Egon Albrecht	4	P		Bf 110 C-4	45%	Crash-landing due to bad ground conditions.	Krasnodar.
	Uffz. Kurt Urban	4	Bf					
	Fw. Hans Papp	4	Bm					
20-12-42		2			Bf 110 E	15%	Belly-landing.	Tazinskaja.
					2312			
20-12-42	Ofw. Wilhelm Dibowski	5	P	W	Bf 110 E-2		Both crewmen wounded on combat mission.	South-east of
	Uffz. Kurt Meier	5	Bf	W	S9+NP			Gramoslawka.
	(5th Staffel crew in a 6th Staffel machine)				3009			
21-12-42		5			Bf 110 E	90%	Hit by Flak.	Werchneslonowski.
					2639			
21-12-42	Fw. Ruland Zahn	6	P	W	Bf 110	90%	Hit by Flak.	
					3733			
22-12-42		2			Bf 110	100%	Hit by Flak.	
					4392			
22-12-42	Hptm. Heinrich Saß	8	P	K	Me 210 A-1	100%	Aircraft crashed on take-off for combat mission.	Trapani airfield.
	(Staffelkapitän)				2N+GS			
	Fw. Rudolf Blasndowski	8	Bf	K	088			
	(Hptm. Harald Zimmermann was killed on the ground by the aircraft's exploding bombs.)							
23-12-42	Uffz. Klaus Leibrant	11	P	W	Me 210 A-1	100%	Both crew wounded on combat mission in combat	15 Kms. from Sousse.
	Uffz. Heinz Zobel	11	Bf	W	2N+BV		with fighters.	
					062			
24-12-42	Fw. Peter Glas	6	P	K	Bf 110 A		Both crew killed on non-combat flight.	Ssalsk airfield.
	Uffz. Christian Rebmann	6	Bf	K	KF+EW			
					4313			
25-12-42	Fw. Ludwig Lutz	4	P	K	Bf 110 C-4		Both crew killed on non-combat flight.	Kirowograd-Peromaisk.
	Prüf-Meister Willi Bender	Stab	Passenger	K	S9+KM			
	Hptm. Günther Dolling	4	Passenger	K	2139			
26-12-42		2			Bf 110 E	30%	Hit by ground fire.	Millerowo.
					4025			
26-12-42		III. Gruppe			Me 210 A-1	10%	Ground-looped during landing.	Trapani.
					062			
27-12-42	Lt. Rudolf Petersen	Stab,	P	K	Bf 110		Crashed on take-off.	Krasnodar airfield.
	Uffz. Ernst Schönfelder	II. Gruppe	Bf	K	S9+IC			
					4603			
27-12-42		11			Me 210 A-1	20%	Ground looped during landing.	Chinisia airfield.
					077			
28-12-42		II. Gruppe			Bf 110 F	75%	Damaged due to icy conditions.	Sochachty-Nord airfield.
					4605			
29-12-42		2			Bf 110		Hit by Flak.	
					4253			
30-12-42		II. Gruppe			Kl 35	90%	Taxied into an obstruction.	Rostow-West airfield.
					3071			
30-12-42		10			Bf 110 F	45%	Hit by Flak.	
					5062			
31-12-42	Uffz. Bruno Baumeister	2	P		Bf 110	100%	Hit by Flak.	
	Uffz. Heinz Ludwig	2	Bf		S9+CK			
					050			
31-12-42	Uffz. Hans Bumber	10	Bf		Bf 110 F-2	40%	Hit by Flak.	
					5061			
05-01-43		3			Bf 110	45%	Engine damage.	Makryj-Log
					3456			
06-01-43		II. Gruppe			Bf 110 F	100%	Bomb explosion.	Schachty airfield.
					5130			
08-01-43	Lt. Erich Le Claire	Stab	P	K	Bf 110 E-1	100%	Shot down on combat mission.	South-west of
	Fw. Ernst Frank	4	Bf	K	S9+JP			Ssemikarakorskaja
					4493			
08-01-43	Fw. Gerhard Schlee	1	Bf	W	Bf 110 D	100%	Hit by Flak.	
					3161			
08-01-43	Fw. Hans Volkery	6	P	W	Bf 110 E-1		Wounded on combat mission.	5 Kms. west
					S9+GM			of Bolschoj.
					3424			

Date	Name of crew and rank	Staffel	Status	Fate	Aircraft code & W.Nr.	Damage state	Reason for casualty	Place
10-01-43	Lt. Henning Niederehe Uffz. Klaus Seifert	6 6	P Bf	M M	Bf 110 E-1 S9+IP 4402	100%	Shot down by Flak on combat mission.	Nishnyi-Wjasowyi.
10-01-43	Oblt. Oskar Genrich Oblt. Otto Crotzmann	II. Gruppe	P P	K K			Passengers in Ju 86 G of K.Gr.z.b.V. 22 which crashed.	Near Proskurow airfield.
15-01-43		III. Gruppe			Me 210 A-1 131	30%		Lecce.
17-01-43	Uffz. Otto Ehrmann	5	Bf	K	Bf 110 E2/U-4 S9+FN 3758		Bordfunker killed on combat mission.	1Km. north of Harkowka.
17-01-43		5			Bf 110 F 5094	20%	Engine problems.	Schachty.
20-01-43	Uffz. Herbert Hoffmann 5060	10	Bf	W	Bf 110 F	65%	Crash-landing.	Schachty,
21-01-43	Lt. Peter Jenne Fw. Alfons Jehle	1 1	P Bf	W K	Bf 110 G-2 S9+GB 5147	50%	Overturned on landing.	Schackty.
21-01-43	Lt. Horst-Joachim Draeger Fw. Helmut Lange	3 3	P Bf	K K	Bf 110 G-2 S9+BL 5143	100%	Shot down by Flak on combat mission.	North of Kamensk.
21-01-43	Ofw. Johann Gruber Uffz. Karl-Heinz Koch	5 Stab	P Bf	M M	Bf 110 E-2 S9+PM 4522	100%	Shot down by Flak on combat mission.	Kamensk.
21-01-43	Fw. Reinhold Miehlke	5	P	W	Bf 110 E/U-3 S9+PP 3811		Pilot wounded on non-combat flight.	Pawlowka.
21-01-43		5			Bf 110 E 3856	45%	Crash-landing.	Schachty.
21-01-43		10			Bf 110 5064	35%	Hit by ground fire.	Schachty.
22-01-43		III. Gruppe			Me 210 A-1 0751	80%	Servicing fault.	Lecce.
30-01-43	Oblt. Eduard Tratt Fw. Paul Rennefahrt	1 1	P Bf	W K	Bf 110 RH+YK 5198	100%	Right engine hit by enemy fire. Both crewmen baled out.	15 Kms. north of Rowenki.
01-02-43	Uffz. Oswald Wawrowicz	9	P	K	Me 210 A-1 078		Crashed on low level flight.	4 Kms. north-east of Bronte.
03-02-43	Fw. Walter Ihmann	4	Bf	W	Bf 110 G-2 S9+SM 5209		Wounded on combat mission.	Kalinin-West.
05-02-43	Uffz. Otto Kühne Uffz. Walter Gauch Gefr. Georg Kießling	I. Gruppe I. Gruppe I. Gruppe	P Bf Bs	K K W	Fw 58 309	100%	Crashed as a result of enemy fire.	South-east of Ssytschewen.
09-02-43		III. Gruppe			C 445 700	10%	Engine trouble.	Lecce.
10-02-43	Uffz. Erich Gralla	9	Bm	K	Me 210 A-1 197	100%	Baled out of aircraft, but fell to his death.	St. Pancration.
10-02-43		III. Gruppe			Me 210 A-1 099	10%	Engine trouble,	Galatone.
11-02-43		III. Gruppe			Me 210 A-1 056	10%	Engine trouble.	Lecce.
13-02-43	Fw. Hans Raum Uffz. Günther-Harald Kowalski	4 4	P Bf		Bf 110 E-2 4432	80%	Emergency landing due to bad weather.	Gerlowka.
13-02-43	Gefr. Albert Kersten	III. Gruppe			Me 210 A-1 223	55%	Overturned.	Chinisia.
13-02-43		III. Gruppe			Me 210 A-1 2311	10%	Ground looped while landing.	Chinisia.
16-02-43		III. Gruppe			Me 210 A-1/Trop 2290	15%	Ground looped while landing.	Chinisia.
24-02-43	Uffz. Josef Scheidler	4	P	W	Bf 110 D-2 3394	80%	Belly-landing following combat damage.	Ssinelikowo.
24-02-43	Uffz. Franz Newesely	4	Bf	W	Bf 110 G-2 S9+UM 5225		Bordfunker wounded on combat mission.	Dobrowolje.
24-02-43		6			Bf 110 E-1 2554	100%	Direct hit from Flak.	
27-02-43	Uffz. Günther Longerich Uffz. Erwin Salomon	4 4	P Bf	M M	Bf 110 G-2 S9+GM 5218	100%	Did not return from combat mission.	Nowo-Ssemenowka.
27-02-43	Uffz. Rudolf Edelbauer Fw. Otto Hierweger	4 4	P Bf	K K	Bf 110 F-2 S9+CM 4537	100%	Did not return from combat mission.	Nowo-Ssemenowka.
27-02-43	Lt. Friedrich Mür	5	P	W	Bf 110 E-1 4098	100%	Shot down in combat.	
27-02-43		III. Gruppe			Me 210 A-1 064	10%	Undercarriage damage.	Chinisia.
27-02-43		III. Gruppe			Bf 110 F-2/Trop 5164	30%	Engine damage.	Trapani.
27-02-43		10			Bf 110 5140	45%	Damaged while taxi-ing.	Bagerowo.

Date	Name of crew and rank	Staffel	Status	Fate	Aircraft code & W.Nr.	Damage state	Reason for casualty	Place
28-02-43		5			Bf 110 D-3 3719	15%	Crash-landing.	Dnjepropetrowsk-Sud airfield.
28-02-43	Uffz. Rolf Etzkorn Uffz. Siegfried Puls	6 6	P Bf	W W	Bf 110 E-1 S9+KM 4083		Both crewmen wounded on combat mission.	6 Km. north-west of Losowaja.
01-03-43		III. Gruppe			Me 210 A-1/Trop 2290	10%	Damaged while taxiing.	Chinisia.
04-03-43	Lt. Fritx Sax	4	P		Bf 110 G-2 S9+SM 5209		Emergency landing following combat mission.	Dnjepro.
04-03-43		9			Me 210 A-1 2N+LT 205	40%	Ran off runway and crashed into wall.	Lecce.
05-03-43	Lt. Arnhold Dorka	5	P	W	Bf 110 G-2 5201	50%	Crashed following combat mission.	
05-03-43		6			Bf 110 E-1 4045	100%	Engine fire.	Taranowa.
05-03-43		10			Bf 110 F 5056		Damaged while taxi-ing.	Bagerowo.
06-03-43	Fw. Josef Kuhlenkamp	4	Bf	W	Bf 110 G-2 S9+FM 5204		Wounded on combat mission.	Dnjepropetrowsk-Süd airfield.
06-03-43	Uffz. Gottfried Häring Uffz. Ernst Bonnrath	7 7	P Bf	W K	Me 210 A 2N+BD 2314	100%	Crashed following combat with RAF fighters.	50 Kms. north of Gabes.
09-03-43		4			Bf 110 G-2 5009	50%	Engine trouble.	Dnjepropetrowsk-Sud airfield.
10-03-43		6			Bf 110 C-7 2891	50%	Damaged by enemy fire.	
10-03-43		II. Gruppe			Bf 110 G-2 6114	75%	Hit by Flak.	Charkow.
11-03-43	Fw. Thiemann Uffz. Alfred Telitzki *(7th Staffel crew flying an 8th Staffel machine)*	7 7	P Bf	W K	Me 210 A 2N+CS 2316	100%	Emergency landing on sea following combat with RAF fighters.	1Km. north-west of Maritimo island.
12-03-43	Uffz. Josef Dors Gefr. Albert Kersten	7 7	P Bf	K K	Me 210 A 2N+PR 8171	100%	Did not return from combat mission.	North of Etna.
12-03-43	Oblt. Bernhard Paffrath Uffz. Heinz van Lomm	9 9	P Bf	W W	Me 210 A 2N+HT 2325	90%	Engines failed on return from combat mission. Aircraft crash-landed.	Gerbini.
13-03-43	Uffz. Kurt Strixner	12	Bf	W			Wounded by ground fire.	
14-03-43		III. Gruppe			Me 210 A-1 066	10%	Engine trouble.	Santa Ilagio.
17-03-43		III. Gruppe			Me 210 A-1 2336	60%	Emergency landing.	North-west of Gabes.
18-03-43	Uffz. Wilhelm Tögel Uffz. Werner Schultz	3 3	P Bf	K K	Bf 110 E-2 SB+FQ 3794	100%	Hit the ground on a low-level attack against a Russian supply column.	West of the Charkow-Belgorod road.
18-03-43		III. Gruppe			Me 210 A-1 2251	20%	Rammed by Italian aircraft.	Chinisia.
19-03-43		III. Gruppe			Me 210 A-1 042	30%	Technical problem.	Capul, near Naples.
19-03-43		12			Fw 58 2027	20%		Near Brjansk.
20-03-43		2			Bf 110 G-2 5250	10%	Airframe damaged on landing.	Charkow-Nord airfield.
20-03-43	Uffz. Walter Brehm	8	P	W	Me 210 A-1 2N+HS 1835		Wounded on combat mission.	Near Trapani.
20-03-43		III. Gruppe			Me 210 A-1 256	30%	Damaged by AA fire.	Sfax.
21-03-43		3			Bf 110 E-2 4331	15%	Damaged in bombing attack.	Poltawa airfield.
21-03-43		3			Bf 110 G-2 5256	30%	Damaged in bombing attack.	Poltawa airfield.
21-03-43		3			Bf 110 E-2 4363	25%	Damaged in bombing attack.	Poltawa airfield.
21-03-43		I. Gruppe			Bf 110 G-2 6137	10%	Nosed-over on landing.	Charkow-Nord airfield.
22-03-43		III. Gruppe			Me 210 A-1 2281	35%	Damaged while taxiing.	Sfax.
23-03-43	Oblt. Franz Bohuslav Uffz. Willi Bark	1 1	P Bf	K K	Bf 110 G-2 DO+PC 6139	100%	Received direct hit from Flak at a height of 230 m..	Pjatnitzkoje.
24-03-43		IV. Gruppe			Me 210 A-1 051	30%	Force-landed due to enemy fire.	Near Gabes.
24-03-43		12			Fw 58 268	20%	Airframe damage.	Witebsk.

Date	Name of crew and rank	Staffel	Status	Fate	Aircraft code & W.Nr.	Damage state	Reason for casualty	Place
25-03-43	Lt. Siegfried Schmeling Uffz. Heinrich Theissen	1 1	P Bf	K K	Bf 110 G-2 3257	100%	Shot down by Russian Lagg-3 fighter.	West of Bataisk.
25-03-43	Uffz. Alois Slaby	III. Gruppe	Bf	W	Me 210 A-1 216	20%	Overturned while landing.	Chinisia.
28-03-43		III. Gruppe			Me 210 A 2337	20%	Belly-landing.	Sfax.
29-03-43		2			Bf 110 G-2 5259	100%	Hit by Flak.	
29-03-43		III. Gruppe			Me 210 A-1 8162	85%	Damaged in bombing attack on airfield.	Sfax airfield.
29-03-43		III. Gruppe			Me 210 A-1 2301	15%	Damaged in bombing attack on airfield.	Sfax airfield.
29-03-43		III. Gruppe			Me 210 A-1 8172	15%	Damaged in bombing attack on airfield.	Sfax airfield.
29-03-43		III. Gruppe			Me 210 A-1 8157	100%	Destroyed in bombing attack on airfield.	Sfax airfield.
29-03-43		III. Gruppe			Me 210 A-1 8167	80%	Damaged in bombing attack on airfield.	Sfax airfield.
29-03-43		III. Gruppe			Me 210 A-1 2318	10%	Damaged in bombing attack on airfield.	Sfax airfield.
29-03-43		III. Gruppe			Me 210 A-1 8161	90%	Damaged in bombing attack on airfield.	Sfax airfield.
30-03-43		III. Gruppe			Me 210 C-1 8175	10%	Tyre failure.	Chinisia.
30-03-43		III. Gruppe			Me 210 C-1 2264	20%	Damaged in bombing attack on airfield.	Sfax airfield.
30-03-43		3			Bf 110 E-1 4096		Bf 109 landing crashed into machine.	Charkow-Sud airfield.
30-03-43	Fw. Müller	10	P	W	Bf 110 6101	40%	Belly-landing following hits from enemy fighter.	Bagerowo.
05-04-43		II. Gruppe			Bf 110 G-2 7131	70%	Damaged in bombing attack.	
05-04-43		II. Gruppe			Bf 110 G-2 4182	70%	Damaged in bombing attack.	
05-04-43		II. Gruppe			Bf 110 G-2 6173	70%	Damaged in bombing attack.	
05-04-43	Ofw. Herbert Hendrich Uffz. Rudolf Kaiser	III. Gruppe III. Gruppe	P Bf	M M	Me 210 2N+FS 5134	100%		Near Gabes.
05-04-43		III. Gruppe			Me 210 C 4177	25%	Damaged in bombing attack on airfield.	Trapani airfield.
05-04-43		III. Gruppe			Me 210 A-1 218	50%	Damaged in bombing attack on airfield.	Chinisia airfield.
05-04-43		III. Gruppe			Me 210 A-1 2268	20%	Damaged in bombing attack on airfield.	Chinisia airfield.
05-04-43		III. Gruppe			Me 210 A-1 2315	10%	Damaged in bombing attack on airfield.	Chinisia airfield.
05-04-43		III. Gruppe			Me 210 A-1 250		Damaged in bombing attack on airfield.	Chinisia airfield.
06-04-43		1			Bf 110 G-2 5223	30%	Airframe damaged on landing.	Kramatorskaja.
06-04-43	Oblt. Rudolf Thomas Uffz. Franz Peters	2 2	P Bf	W	Bf 110 G-2 6118	100%	Engine hit; both crew baled out. Both returned to unit.	
06-04-43		2			Bf 110 G-2 4601	40%	Damaged by enemy fire.	Krementschug.
06-04-43	Uffz. Gerhard Lemke Uffz. Emil Dolch	9 9	P Bf	M M	Me 210 A-1 2N+JT 092	100%	Did not return from combat mission.	30 Kms. north-west of Gabes.
06-04-43	Uffz. Walter Lübke Uffz. Rudolf Hüttner	9 9	P Bf	M M	Me 210 A-1 2N+BR 170	100%	Did not return from combat mission.	30 Kms. north-west of Gabes.
06-04-43		III. Gruppe			Me 210 A-1 5214	50%	Engine trouble.	Biserta.
06-04-43		III. Gruppe			Me 210 A-1 0029	100%	Destroyed by own troops.	
09-04-43	Uffz. Gerhard Melhorn Uffz. Otto Sparrer	8 8	P Bf	M M	Me 210 A-1 2N+MS 265	100%	Did not return from combat mission.	2 Kms. north of Bou Thadi.
09-04-43		III. Gruppe			Me 210 A-1 2297	70%	Damaged by enemy fighter.	Near Kairouan.
10-04-43	Lt. Rudi Dassow Uffz. Walter Böhme	7 7	P Bf	 K	Me 210 A-1 2N+GR 8169	100%	Aircraft did not return from combat mission. Lt. Dassow returned to the unit on 16.04.43.	North-west of Bou Thadi.
10-04-43	Lt. Wedig-Bog von Glasenapp Uffz. Martin Schretzenmeyer	7 7	P Bf	W W	Me 210 A-1 8170	100%	Both crewmen wounded on combat mission. Aircraft a write-off.	10 Kms. north of Kroussian-Sahali.
10-04-43		7			Me 210 A-1 8160	20%	Damage as a result of combat.	Kappon coast.
10-04-43	Oblt. Josef Halterbach	9	P	W	Me 210 C-1 2276	100%	Casualty due to enemy fire.	Near Sousse.

Date	Name of crew and rank	Staffel	Status	Fate	Aircraft code & W.Nr.	Damage state	Reason for casualty	Place
10-04-43		9			Me 210 C-1 2326	100%	Shot down by enemy fire. Crew unhurt.	
10-04-43		9			Me 210 A-1 2296	100%	Shot down by enemy fire. Crew unhurt.	
12-04-43		2			Bf 110 G-2 6123	30%	Damaged by enemy fire.	Poltawa.
12-04-43		III. Gruppe			Me 210 A-1 220	30%	Ground looped during landing.	Chinisia.
14-04-43		III. Gruppe			Me 210 A-1 2289	100%	Emergency landing on sea due to engine damage.	
15-04-43	Oblt. Thüring Ogefr. Hemenstein	III. Gruppe III. Gruppe	P Bf	W W	Me 210 A-1 183	100%	Emergency landing due to engine damage.	Gerbini.
16-04-43		III. Gruppe			Me 210 A-1 064	15%	Ground looped during take-off.	Chinisia.
17-04-43	Uffz. Franz Böck Uffz. Henry Ahrens *(6th Staffel crew flying a machine of 7./ZG 26)*	6 6	P Bf	W K	Bf 110 G-2/ Trop 3U+SR 5122	100%	Shot down into the Mediterranean Sea.	Between Tunis and Sicily.
17-04-43		III. Gruppe			Me 210 A-1 095	15%	Damaged by enemy fighter.	
17-04-43		III. Gruppe			Me 210 A-1 1052	35%	Belly-landed following enemy action.	
17-04-43		III. Gruppe			Me 210 A-1 2288	35%	Belly-landed following enemy action.	
19-04-43		10			Bf 110 G-2 6134	30%	Servicing fault.	Bagerowo.
20-04-43	Flgr. Heinz Behnke	3	Bf	W	Bf 110 E-2 S9+OL 3756	20%	Damaged on combat mission.	Kramatorskaja.
20-04-43		10			Bf 110 G-2 5146	80%	Crashed on take-off.	Bagerowo.
21-04-43		1			Bf 110 F-2 5131	20%	Airframe damage.	Kramatorskaja.
23-04-43		7			Me 210 A-1 2286	10%	Crash-landing.	Chinisia.
25-04-43	Oblt. Alexander Gibsone Uffz. Otto Weissflog	6 6	P Bf	M M	Bf 110 G-2/ Trop S9+TP 6189	100%	Did not return from combat mission.	Straits of Sicily.
26-04-43		3			Bf 110 E-2 3781	30%	Engine trouble.	
26-04-43	Oblt. Günther Schmidt Uffz. Karl-Heinz Kölzow	I. Gruppe I. Gruppe	P Bf		Bf 110 F-2 2698	80%	Direct hit from Flak.	Artemowsk.
27-04-43		10			Bf 110 F 5058	75%	Crash-landing.	Bagerowo.
28-04-43		3			Bf 110 E-2 4331	70%	Hit by Flak.	Kramatorskaja.
28-04-43		III. Gruppe			Fi 156 8133	30%	Overturned on landing.	Taormina.
29-04-43	Uffz. Gerhard Czach	3	Bf	W	Bf 110 E-2 S9+OL 3756		Wounded by ground fire from Russian troops. Died two days later.	South of Petrowka.
30-04-43	Lt. Fritz Lyos	1	P	W	Bf 110 F-2 4554	30%	Damaged on combat mission.	Kramatorskaja.
30-04-43		III. Gruppe			Bf 110 G-2 5199	20%	Crash-landing.	Trapani.
01-05-43	Oblt. Kurt Eiffländer Fw. Heinz Rumke *(4th Staffel crew flying a Stab, II. Gruppe machine)*	4 4	P Bf	M M	Bf 110 G-2/ Trop S9+AC 6163	100%	Did not return following combat with British fighters.	Cap Bon.
01-05-43	Ogefr. Werner Hess Uffz. Hubert Assmann *(4th Staffel crew flying a Stab, II. Gruppe machine)*	4 4	P Bf	M M	Bf 110 G-2/ Trop S9+BC 6238	100%	Did not return following combat with British fighters.	Cap Bon.
01-05-43	Ofw. Georg Stengel Uffz. Werner Hellwig	4 4	P Bf	M M	Bf 110 G-2/ Trop S9+CM 6190	100%	Did not return following combat with British fighters.	Cap Bon.
01-05-43	Lt. Georg Meyer Uffz. Erich Finze	6 6	P Bf	M M	Bf 110 G-2/ Trop S9+IP 6178	100%	Seen to crash into the sea on combat mission.	Straits of Sicily.
02-05-43	Fw. Werner Menard Uffz. Kurt Walter	3 3	P Bf	K M	Bf 110 G-2 S9+XL 6203	100%	Direct hit from Flak. Bordfunker seen to bail out.	Nowoderkul.
03-05-43		II. Gruppe			Bf 110 G-2 6151	100%	Junkers 52 crashed into machine.	Trapani.
05-05-43		II. Gruppe			Bf 110 G-2 6183	80%	Tyre damage.	Trapani.

Date	Name of crew and rank	Staffel	Status	Fate	Aircraft code & W.Nr.	Damage state	Reason for casualty	Place
09-05-43	Lt. Wolfgang Priebe Fw. Friedrich Kleine-Kleffmann	4 4	P Bf	W K	Bf 110 G-2/ Trop S9+MM 6237	100%	Crashed following combat mission.	20 Kms. south-south-east of Reggio.
10-05-43	Fw. Herbert Dentzer Uffz. Werner Schult	2 2	P Bf	M M	Bf 110 G-2 S9+CK 5216	100%	Hit by Flak and Russian fighter and crashed.	East of Russkt-Brod.
10-05-43	Oblt. Ferdinand Glanz Ofw. Hermann Schalow	9 9	P Bf	W W	Me 210 A 2N+NT 8174		Both crewmen wounded on combat mission.	15 Kms. north-north-east of Catania.
11-05-43		1			Bf 110 F-4 4604	70%	Crash-landed due to airframe damage.	Lodna-Ost airfield.
11-05-43		III. Gruppe			Me 210 A-1 0252	35%	Airframe damaged on landing.	München-Oberwiesenfeld airfield.
11-05-43		10			Bf 110 G-2 6247	20%	Servicing fault.	Bagerowo.
12-05-43	Uffz. Günther Kobe	12	P	K	Arado 66 897	100%	Shot down by own Flak.	East of Matschuliniki.
16-05-43	Oblt. Hans-Erich Hesse Uffz. Paul Kastner	3 3	P Bf	K K	Bf 110 G-2 S9+DL 6244	100%	Aircraft received direct hit from Flak during attack on Schtschgry airfield.	Schtschgry.
21-05-43	Uffz. Joachim Nitschalk Gefr. Walter Hofbauer	8 8	P Bf	M M	Me 210 A-1 2N+LS 2313	100%	Did not return from reconnaissance mission.	Cap Bon.
23-05-43	Lt. Erich Holthuis	5	P	M	Bf 110 G-2/ Trop S9+KN 6155	100%	Crashed into the sea on combat mission.	24 Kms. east of Soverato.
24-05-43	Lt. Hubert Reichelt	10	P	W	Bf 110 G-2 6261	90%	Crashed due to engine problems.	Bagerowo.
24-05-43	Oblt. Wilhelm Wippenhorst Hptm. Karl Kahul Sdfhr. Max Lengwenings	10 10 Bb	P Bf K	K K	Bf 110 G-2 6135	100%	Aircraft crashed - cause not known.	
28-05-43		Gesch. Stab			Bf 110 E-1 4049	40%	Engine damage.	South-west of Gremjatsch.
28-05-43	Fw. Heinz Melchert Uffz. Heinz Garthein	10 10	P		Bf 110 G-2 2N+PU 6258	100%	Shot down in combat.	Krymskaja.
30-05-43	Uffz. Heinz Wäterling	9	Bf	W	Me 210 A 2N+KT 225		Bordfunker wounded on combat mission.	80 Kms. south-west of Maritimo island.
30-05-43		III. Gruppe			Me 210 A-1 2298	100%	Emergency landing following combat mission.	Near Maritimo.
01-06-43		III. Gruppe			Me 210 A-1 083	80%	Engine problem.	South-east of Gerbini.
01-06-43		II. Gruppe			Me 210 6188	70%	Tyre failure.	Praitca di Mare.
02-06-43	Oblt. Günther Schmidt Uffz. Karl-Heinz Kölzow	1 1	P Bf	W W	Bf 110 F-2 5133	100%	Emergency landing. Aircraft burnt out.	Bogorodizkije.
02-06-43	Uffz. Johann Lonzek Uffz. Hans-Horst Kelch	3 3	P Bf	K K	Bf 110 G-2 S9+VL 6127	100%	Shot down by Russian fighters.	Ghotrowo.
02-06-43		3			Bf 110 G-2 5212	70%	Crash-landing following combat mission.	Ledna-Ost airfield.
02-06-43	Lt. Gerhard Scheer Uffz. Willi Hartmann *(9th Staffel pilot flying an 8th Staffel aircraft)*	9 9	P Bf	W W	Me 210 A 2N+MS 241		Crew wounded on combat mission.	South of Sicily.
02-06-43	Lt. Otto-Karl Raden	III. Gruppe	P	W	Fi 156 C-3/ Trop 4083	20%	Technical problem.	Gela.
02-06-43					Bf 110 F-2 2701	50%	Crash-landing following combat mission.	Ledna-Ost airfield.
06-06-43	Fw. Arthur Rostek Gefr. Willi Bennecke	1 1	P Bf	M M	Bf 110 S9+IH 5055	100%	Did not return from combat mission.	15 Kms. north-east of Schtschgry.
11-06-43		III. Gruppe			Me 210 A-1 087	100%	Destroyed by bombing attack.	Castel Vetrano airfield.
12-06-43		III. Gruppe			Me 210 259	10%		
20-06-43	Uffz. Johann Lameraner Gefr. Josef Görthofer	1 1	P Bf	K K	Bf 110 S9+UH 4535	100%	Shot down by Flak on combat mission.	2 Kms. south of Belew.
20-06-43	Lt. Rigobert Benold Uffz. Ernst Mittrowann	2 2	P Bf	M M	Bf 110 G-2 S9+BK 5197	100%	Force-landed on Russian side of lines on combat mission.	
20-06-43		III. Gruppe			Me 210 A-1 156	70%	Damaged in bombing attack.	Castel Vetrano airfield.
23-06-43		III. Gruppe			Me 210 A-1 2310	80%	Engine problem.	South of Vicenza.

Date	Name of crew and rank	Staffel	Status	Fate	Aircraft code & W.Nr.	Damage state	Reason for casualty	Place
24-06-43	Uffz. Werner Günther Gefr. Hugo Ludwig	9 9	P Bf	M M	Me 210 A-1 2N+JT 063	100%		
27-06-43		10			Bf 110 G-2 6138	25%	Damaged while taxi-ing.	Saporoshje-Ost airfield.
01-07-43		II. Gruppe			Bf 110 G-2/ Trop 6212	25%	Airframe damage.	Ciampino-Nord airfield.
05-07-43		Gesch. Stab			Bf 110 G-2 6298	30%	Crash-landing due to servicing fault.	Ledna-Ost airfield.
05-07-43		I. Gruppe			Bf 110 G-2 6129	80%	Belly landing following engine damage.	Kagino.
05-07-43		3			Bf 110 E-2 4329	20%	Crash-landing.	Ledna-Ost airfield.
06-07-43	Uffz. Willi Welkisch Uffz. Heinz Vogler	3 3	P Bf	K M	Bf 110 S9+VL 3845	100%	Shot down by Russian fighters on combat mission.	Ssamodurowka.
06-07-43		II. Gruppe			Bf 110 G-2/ Trop 6232	45%	Crash-landing.	Montecorvino.
09-07-43		Pz. Jg. St. ZG 1			Bf 110 G-2 6290	40%	Technical problems.	Ledna-Ost airfield.
10-07-43	Ofw. Ernst Klebert	1	P	K	Bf 110 G-2 S9+HH 6119	100%	Direct hit from Flak. Bordfunker baled out and returned to unit.	North of Kutürky.
10-07-43		2			Bf 110 G-2 5250	65%	Belly-landing following combat damage.	Sinmanka.
10-07-43		II.			Bf 110 G-2/ Trop 6234	80%	Hit by Flak.	Montecorvino.
11-07-43	Stfw. Paul Rapp Fw. Gerhard Freyer	4 4	P Bf	K	Bf 110 G-2 S9+DM 6191		Hit by Flak and attacked by 3 British fighters. Crash-landed.	15 Kms. south-east of Mazzarino.
11-07-43	Uffz. Franz Hillmann Uffz. Josef Jauernik	4 4	P Bf	W W	Bf 110 G-2/Trop S9+EM 6153			Gela.
11-07-43	Fw. Hermann Gerdes	5	P	W	Bf 110 G-2 S9+BN 6172		Pilot killed on combat mission.	10 Kms. east of Gela.
11-07-43	Uffz. Richard Blind	5	Bf	K	Bf 110 G-2 S9+KN 6301		Bordfunker killed on combat mission.	15 Kms. east of Gela.
11-07-43	Oblt. Wilhelm Dreher Uffz. Oskar Stellmacher	II. Gruppe II. Gruppe	P Bf		Bf 110 G-2 6181	100%	Reason for loss not known.	Gela.
12-07-43	Uffz. Rudolf Müller Gefr. Karl Forsthuber	1 1	P Bf	M M	Bf 110 G-2 S9+FH 6113	100%	Shot down in combat with Russian fighters.	North of Uljanowo.
12-07-43	Fw. Reinhold Miehlke Uffz. Horst Wiese	5 5	P Bf	K	Bf 110 G-2/ Trop S9+GN 6152		Pilot killed following direct hit from Flak on combat mission.	10 Kms. south-west of Licodia.
12-07-43		II. Gruppe			Bf 110 C-1 0945	40%	Bombing attack.	Montecorvino.
12-07-43		II. Gruppe			Bf 110 G-2/ Trop 6299	100%	Bombing attack.	Montecorvino.
12-07-43		II. Gruppe			Bf 110 G-2/ Trop 6217	50%	Belly-landing due to combat damage.	
13-07-43	Obstlt. Joachim Blechschmidt (Geschwaderkommodore) Uffz. Hans Wörl	Gesch. Stab Gesch. Stab	P Bf	M M	Bf 110 G-2 S9+BA 6295	100%	Force-landed behind Russian lines following combat with Russian fighters. Both crewmen seen to leave the aircraft.	Uljanowo-Bolchow.
13-07-43		2			Bf 110 G-2 6111	25%	Damaged by enemy fire.	Near Uljanowo.
13-07-43		3			Bf 110 G-2 6292	15%	Technical problem.	Sljanowe-Bolchoff.
13-07-43	Lt. Werner Mihatsch Uffz. Harry Weiß	Pz. Jg. St. ZG 1 Pz. Jg. St. ZG 1	P Bf	W M	Bf 110 G-2 6252	100%	Hit by Flak.	West of Gorodok.
14-07-43	Hptm. Wilfried Herrmann (Gruppenkommandeur) Ofw. Albert Weinhold	Stab, I. Gruppe Stab, I. Gruppe	P Bf	K K	Bf 110 G-2 S9+FB 6327	100%	Received direct hit from Flak on combat mission.	Krapiwna.
14-07-43	Uffz. Willi Matschiowalli Uffz. Hans Westermann	3 3	P Bf	K K	Bf 110 F-2 S9+TH 5107	100%	Received direct hit from Flak on combat mission.	3 Kms. south-west of Krapiwna.
14-07-43		2			Bf 110 G-2 6297	100%	Belly-landing following hits by fighters.	Lumwko.

Date	Name of crew and rank	Staffel	Status	Fate	Aircraft code & W.Nr.	Damage state	Reason for casualty	Place
14-07-43		Pz. Jg. St. ZG 1			Bf 110 G-2 6295	15%	Technical problem.	Ledna-Ost airfield.
14-07-43	Uffz. Kurt Dames	Pz. Jg. St. ZG 1	Bf		Bf 110 G-2 6289	70%	Belly-landing after hit by Flak.	West of Kosjulcina.
14-07-43	Uffz. Herbert Stengel Uffz. Adolf Heusinger	Pz. Jg. St. ZG 1 Pz. Jg. St. ZG 1	P Bf	W K	Bf 110 F-2 5202	100%	Hit by Flak. Burnt out on ground.	West of Kosjulcina.
15-07-43		7			Me 210 A-1 279	30%	Emergency landing due to technical failure.	Antwerp.
17-07-43	Uffz. Karl Sünderhauff	4	Bf	K	Bf 110 G-2 S9+GM 6148		Bordfunker killed on combat mission.	Near Capri.
17-07-43	Uffz. Erich Essig Uffz. Rudolf Beilner	5 5	P Bf	K K	Bf 110 G-2 S9+EN 6143		Both crewmen killed on combat mission.	5 Kms. west of Montecorvino airfield.
18-07-43	Lt. Siegfried Hamisch	2	P	K	Bf 110 S9+KK 6120	100%	Left engine hit by Flak. Crashed behind German lines. Bordfunker unhurt.	Selotarewo.
18-07-43		2			Bf 110 G-2 5256	20%	Airframe damaged on landing.	Ledna-Ost airfield.
19-07-43	Hptm. Max Franzisket Fw. Harri Pittack	Stab, I. Gruppe	P Bf	M M	Bf 110 S9+BB 6361	100%	Received direct hit from Flak on combat mission.	
19-07-43		2			Bf 110 G-2 5207	25%	Belly-landing following hits from fighters.	Ledna-Ost airfield.
19-07-43	Fw. Bernhardt Grundt Uffz. Kurt Geyer	5 5	P Bf	 M	Bf 110 G-2/ Trop S9+CN 6229	100%	Collided with S9+EM during combat with Spitfires.	20 Kms. north of Taormina.
19-07-43	Uffz. Franz Hillmann Uffz. Josef Jauernick	4 4	P Bf	M M	Bf 110 G-2/ Trop S9+EM 6153	100%	Collided with S9+CN during combat with Spitfires.	20 Kms. north of Taormina.
20-07-43	Fw. Gotthard Wagner Uffz. Hellmut Schranz	1 1	P Bf	W W	Bf 110 S9+KH 5132		Hit by Flak in right engine; aircraft crash-landed.	Zukanowka.
20-07-43		II. Gruppe			Bf 110 G-2/ Trop S9+GM 6148	100%	Destroyed in bombing attack.	Montecorvino.
20-07-43		II. Gruppe			Bf 110 G-2/ Trop 6161	75%	Damaged in bombing attack.	Montecorvino.
20-07-43		II. Gruppe			Bf 110 G-2/ Trop 6185	90%	Damaged in bombing attack.	Montecorvino.
20-07-43		II. Gruppe			Bf 110 G-2/ Trop 6187	60%	Damaged in bombing attack.	Montecorvino.
21-07-43	Fw. Max Wetzel	1	P	W	Bf 110 F-2 2698	80%	Overturned on landing.	Trossna airfield.
22-07-43	Uffz. Wilhelm Kreutzinger	3	P	K	Bf 110 S9+CL 5210	100%	Direct hit from Flak. Bordfunker baled out and returned to unit.	
22-07-43		3			Bf 110 G-2 5614	70%	Belly-landed due to servicing fault.	Ledna-Ost airfield.
22-07-43		I. Gruppe			Fi 156 C-3/ Trop 1206	15%	Belly-landed due to servicing fault.	Ledna-Ost airfield.
22-07-43	Fw. Walter Purrmann Uffz. Alexander Zavelberg	10 10	P Bf	K K	Bf 110 E-2 2648	100%	Crashed due to engine fire.	North of Bagerowo.
22-07-43		Pz. Jg. St. ZG 1			Bf 110 G-2 5236	30%	Belly-landing due to servicing fault.	Brjansk airfield.
23-07-43	Oblt. Heinz Hogeweg Uffz. Konrad Aust	3 3	P Bf	M M	Bf 110 S9+BL 6379	100%	Hit by Flak on combat mission. Crash-landed behind enemy lines.	South-east of Orel.
25-07-43	Lt. Alfred Erler Uffz. Alfred Reinsch	2 2	P Bf	W W	Bf 110 G-2 S9+BK 5612	100%	Hit by Flak on combat mission. Both crewmen baled out.	
26-07-43		7			Me 410 A-1 0046	30%	Airframe damaged while taxi-ing.	Brest-Sud airfield.
27-07-43		3			Fi 156 C-3/ Trop 1105	35%	Damaged while taxi-ing.	Wittmundhafen.
27-07-43		I. Gruppe			Bf 110 G-2 6121	25%	Belly-landing due to engine damage.	North of Orel.
28-07-43	Fw. Karl Hirschmann Uffz. Günther-Harald Kowalski	4 4	P Bf	K K	Bf 110 G-2/ Trop S9+AM 5632	100%	Shot down in combat with fighters during attack on shipping.	North-east of Catania.

Date	Name of crew and rank	Staffel	Status	Fate	Aircraft code & W.Nr.	Damage state	Reason for casualty	Place
30-07-43	Ofw. Wilhelm Büschen	8	P	W			Pilot wounded on combat mission.	German Bight.
31-07-43	Ogefr. Alfred Schwarz	I. Gruppe	P	W	Bf 110 G-2 5205	35%	Damaged while taxi-ing.	Wittmundhafen.
02-08-43		2			Bf 110 G-2 5631	10%	Belly-landing.	Wunsdorf airfield.
02-08-43	Major Heinz Nacke (Gruppenkommandeur)	Stab, II. Gruppe	P	W	Bf 110 G-2 S9+KM		Crashed on non-combat flight.	
	Ofw. Hans-Joachim Kobel	Stab, II.		W	6303			
	Uffz. Anton Maigler	Gruppe		W				
02-08-43		II. Gruppe			Bf 110 G-2 6403	20%	Damaged by obstruction on airfield.	Memmingen airfield.
02-08-43					Bf 110 G-2 6403	20%	Damaged by obstruction on airfield.	Memmingen airfield.
07-08-43		10			Bf 110 G-2 6393	75%	Belly-landing.	Bagerowo airfield.
14-08-43		10			Bf 110 G-2 6389	45%	Airframe damage.	Bagerowo airfield.
20-08-43		2			Bf 110 G-2 6125	25%	Emergency landing after running out of fuel.	Neuenfelde.
20-08-43		I. Gruppe			Bf 110 G-2 6725	30%	Emergency landing after running out of fuel.	Elsfleth.
20-08-43		III. Gruppe			Me 410 A-1 047	80%	Engine damage.	Quakenbrück.
21-08-43	Uffz. Georg Planer	5	P	K	Bf 110 G-2	100%	Crashed into the sea during combat with Liberator.	West of Brest.
	Uffz. Horst Hoffmann	5	Bf	K	S9+GN 6406			
21-08-43		III. Gruppe			Junkers W 34 547	20%	Emergency landing due to engine problem.	Near Minden.
23-08-43		II. Gruppe			Bf 110 G-2 6366	10%	Hit by own Flak.	Atlantic Coast.
23-08-43		II. Gruppe			Bf 110 G-2 6332		Belly-landing due to engine trouble.	Brest-Süd airfield.
24-08-43	Lt. Ernst Albert	2	P	W	Bf 110	100%	Crashed on non-combat flight. Both crewmen died	300 m. west
	Uffz. Gerhard Büttner	2	Bf	W	S9+LK 6108		in hospital 3 days later.	of Bordenau.
24-08-43	Uffz. Erwin Kunze	II. Gruppe	Bf	W	Bf 110 G-2 S9+KN 6301		Belly-landing due to engine trouble.	Brest-Süd airfield.
02-09-43	Lt. Dieter Lax	3	P	K	Bf 110 S9+CL 5605	100%	Collided with S9+AL on non-combat flight.	3 Kms. west of Wunsdorf airfield.
02-09-43	Uffz. Werner Böhmerle	3	Bf	K	Bf 110 S9+AL 5617	100%	Collided with S9+CL on non-combat flight.	3 Kms. west of Wunsdorf airfield.
06-09-43	Lt. Heinz Richter	I. Gruppe	P	W	Bf 110 G-2	80%	Emergency landing due to engine trouble.	Osterberg.
	Uffz. Erwin Alb	I. Gruppe	Bf	W	5146			
11-09-43		I. Gruppe			Bf 110 G-2 6380	15%	Damaged while taxi-ing.	Wunsdorf.
11-09-43	Lt. Dieter Bambauer	5	P	K	Bf 110 G-2	100%	Shot down in combat with four Mosquitos.	
	Uffz. Hermann Grotsch	5	Bf	K	S9+EN 6390			
11-09-43		III. Gruppe			Me 410 A-1 233	10%		Vörden airfield.
13-09-43		I. Gruppe			Bf 110 G-2 5638	15%	Belly-landing.	Lippspringe.
16-09-43		II. Gruppe			Bf 110 G-2 6366	15%	Damaged on landing.	Brest-Süd airfield.
19-09-43		III. Gruppe			Me 410 A-1 0116	20%	Damaged while taxi-ing.	Vörden airfield.
24-09-43		I. Gruppe			Bf 110 E 4094	10%	Airframe damaged on take-off.	Memmingen airfield.
24-09-43	Oblt. Arnold Dorka	4	P	M	Bf 110 G-2	100%	Did not return from combat mission.	South-west of Brest.
	Fw. Ernst Bieber	4	Bf	M	S9+KM 6387			
24-09-43	Lt. Franz Schwarz	5	P	M	Bf 110 G-2	100%	Did not return from combat mission.	South-west of Brest.
	Uffz. Erich Reiterer	5	Bf	M	S9+NN 120054			
24-09-43	Oblt. Gottfried Kayl	5	P		Bf 110 G-2	20%	Belly-landing.	Brest airfield.
	Fw. Hans Fuchs	5	Bf		5626			
24-09-43	Ofw. Ruland Zahn	5	P		Bf 110 G-2	100%	Shot down in combat with Spitfires.	
	Fw. Ernst Patzke	5	Bf	K	S9+MN 120070			
24-09-43	Uffz. Nikolaus Schuller	II. Gruppe			Bf 110 G-2 150127	20%	Belly-landing.	Brest airfield.
27-09-43	Uffz. Gerhard Görsch	9	P	K	Me 410	100%	Both engines failed and aircraft crashed.	Near Ahlhorn-Hann
	Uffz. Rudi Ohst	9	Bf	K	2N+CT 113			airfield.
08-10-43	Oblt. Rudiger Ossmann (Staffelkapitän)	1	P	K	Bf 110 G-2 S9+AH	100%	Shot down in combat with British/American bombers.	20 Kms. east of Dümmersee.
	Fw. Georg Müller	1	Bf	K	120047			

Date	Name of crew and rank	Staffel	Status	Fate	Aircraft code & W.Nr.	Damage state	Reason for casualty	Place
08-10-43	Uffz. Theo Göpel	3	P	K	Bf 110 S9+ML 6130	100%	Crashed on non-combat flight. Cause not known.	Neuhaus, Holzminden.
08-10-43	Hptm. Karl-Heinrich Matern (Gruppenkommandeur) Ofw. Helmuth Bitterling *(Gruppen Stab and 5th Staffel crew flying a 6th Staffel aircraft)*	Stab, II. Gruppe 5	P Bf	M M	Bf 110 G-2 S9+RP 120010	100%	Shot down in combat with Spitfires.	West of Brest.
08-10-43	Lt. Hans-Bodo Busch (Gruppenadjutant) Fw. Karl-Arthur Krampe	Stab, II. Gruppe Stab, II. Gruppe	P Bf	M M	Bf 110 G-2 S9+BC 6396	100%	Shot down in combat. Crashed into the sea.	Atlantic Ocean.
08-10-43	Lt. Gerhard Busse Fw. Ludwig Schalk	4 4	P Bf	M M	Bf 110 G-2 S9+EM 150113	100%	Shot down in combat. Crashed into the sea.	Atlantic Ocean.
08-10-43	Lt. Wolfgang Priebe Uffz. Peter Kühl *(4th Staffel crew flying a 5th Staffel aircraft)*	4 4	P Bf	PoW PoW	Bf 110 G-2 S9+SN 150130	100%	Did not return from combat mission.	
08-10-43	Fw. Herbert Nimtsch Uffz. Helmut Glass *(4th Staffel crew flying a 6th Staffel aircraft)*	4 4	P Bf	M M	Bf 110 G-2 S9+SP 6393	100%	Shot down in combat. Crashed into the sea.	Atlantic Ocean.
08-10-43	Uffz. Julius Reisch Gefr. Richard Sieber	4 4	P Bf	M M	Bf 110 G-2 S9+BP 6395	100%	Shot down in combat. Crashed into the sea.	Atlantic Ocean.
08-10-43	Ofw. Fritz Dotter Uffz. Theodor Gaulrapp *(5th Staffel crew flying a II. Gruppenstab aircraft)*	5 5	P Bf	M M	Bf 110 G-2 S9+AC 6400	100%	Shot down in combat. Crashed into the sea.	Atlantic Ocean.
08-10-43	Lt. Gerhard Thiel Uffz. Josef Schneider *(6th Staffel crew flying a 5th Staffel aircraft)*	6 6	P Bf	K W	Bf 110 G-2 S9+IN 6154		Pilot killed, Bordfunker wounded on combat mission.	South of Brest.
08-10-43	Ogefr. Gerhard Kunde	6	Bf	K	Bf 110 G-2 S9+AP 150132		Bordfunker killed on combat mission.	10 Kms. west of Brest.
08-10-43		II. Gruppe			Bf 110 G-2 6378	100%	Crashed into the sea following combat.	
08-10-43		II. Gruppe			Bf 110 G-2 6204	20%	Belly-landing.	Brest-Süd airfield.
08-10-43		II. Gruppe			Bf 110 G-2 150112	100%	Destroyed in bombing attack.	Brest-Süd airfield.
08-10-43		II. Gruppe			Bf 110 G-2 5628	50%	Damaged in bombing attack.	Brest-Süd airfield.
08-10-43		II. Gruppe			Bf 110 G-2 6175	10%	Damaged in bombing attack.	Brest-Süd airfield.
08-10-43	Uffz. Adolf Wenzel Uffz. Erich Luttkus	7 7	P Bf	W K	Me 410 2N+LR 231		Pilot wounded, Bordfunker killed, on combat mission.	Over Bremen.
08-10-43	Uffz. Günther Sonntag	8	Bf	K	Me 410 2N+FS 020		Bordfunker baled out following combat. Found dead.	Lohne.
09-10-43	Lt. Wolfgang Gümmel Uffz. Wolfgang Skerupka	I. Gruppe I. Gruppe	P Bf	W W	Bf 110 G-2 6376		Damaged in combat.	South of Tondern.
09-10-43	Fw. Willi Schlecht Ofw. Rudolf Müller	I. Gruppe I. Gruppe	P Bf	W K	Me 210 2309	100%	Shot down by friendly fighters.	Kimbrück.
10-10-43		I. Gruppe			Bf 110 G-2 6372	70%	Crash-landed following combat.	Wyk.
10-10-43	Uffz. Ernst Freyer	I. Gruppe		W	Bf 110 G-2 120027		Belly-landing following combat.	Aurich.
10-10-43		I. Gruppe			Bf 110 G-2 6381	25%	Damaged in combat.	Holstedt.
10-10-43	Major Wilhelm Berlin (Gruppenkommandeur) Lt. Heinz Wulf	Stab, III. Gruppe Stab, III. Gruppe	P Bf	K K	Me 410 2N+AD 025	100%	Shot down on combat mission.	Near Osnabrück.
10-10-43	Ofw. Karl Grinninger Fw. Alfred Niehüser	7 7	P Bf	K W	Me 410 A-1 2N+HR 420031	100%	Shot down on combat mission.	Near Lohne.
10-10-43	Oblt. Josef Hallerbach Uffz. Kurt Noae	9 9	P Bf	W K	Me 410 A-1 2N+HT 116		Casualties occurred on combat mission.	Appeldoorn, Holland.
10-10-43	Ofw. Robert Reck Uffz. Ludwig Eisenmann	9 9	P Bf	K K	Me 410 2N+KT 239	100%	Shot down on combat mission.	30 Kms. east-south-east of Osnabrück.
10-10-43		III. Gruppe			Me 410 A-1 112	100%	Crash-landed following combat.	Rheine airfield.
10-10-43		III. Gruppe			Me 410 A-1 027	40%	Damaged in combat.	Twente airfield.
14-10-43	Uffz. Max Wichert Uffz. Kurt Schröder	6 6	P Bf	M K	Bf 110 G-2 S9+TP 150131	100%	Shot down on combat mission. Schröder's body washed ashore on 16/10/43 at Quessant Island.	
14-10-43	Oblt. Heinz Wilhelm (Staffelkapitän)	8	P	K	Me 410 2N+ES	100%	Shot down on combat mission.	7 Kms. south of Werneck.

Date	Name of crew and rank	Staffel	Status	Fate	Aircraft code & W.Nr.	Damage state	Reason for casualty	Place
	Uffz. Günther Herden	8	Bf	K	125			
14-10-43	Fw. August Rosier	III. Gruppe		K	Me 410 0040	100%	Crashed following combat.	Near Frankfurt am Main.
15-10-43		I. Gruppe			Bf 110 G-2 5642	30%	Technical problem.	Near Paderborn.
23-10-43		I. Gruppe			Ju 88 C-6 360358	100%	Emergency landing with engine trouble.	Near Cap du Raz.
25-10-43		II. Gruppe			Me 410 6332	90%	Damaged in bombing attack.	Brest-Süd airfield.
03-11-43	Lt. Hans Schulz	2	P	K	Ju 88 C-6	100%	Crashed on non-combat flight.	Horton, north of
	Ogefr. Roland Dürr	2	Bf	W				Bordeaux-Merignac
	Ogefr. Konstantin Uhde	2	Bb	K				airfield.
20-11-43	Uffz. Christian Böhme	5		W			Aircraft crashed.	Wels.
20-11-43	Oblt. Hans Schuster	7	P	K	Ju 88 C-6	100%	Shot down in combat with Mosquito and Beaufighter.	
	Ofw. Alois Olszowi	7	Bf	K	2N+GL			
	Uffz. Heinrich Bartling	7	Bb	K	360403			
	(III. Gruppe Ju 88 C-6s used I. Gruppe codes for 4th character)							
23-11-43	Ofw. Erich Bindzus	7	P	K	Ju 88 C-6	100%	Collided with Ju 88 C-6 of Fw. Lusser.	10 Kms. north-west of
	Uffz. Werner Geissler	7	Bf	K				Lorient airfield.
	Fw. Karl Weegmann	7	Bb	K				
23-11-43	Fw. Otto Lusser	7	P	K	Ju 88 C-6	100%	Collided with Ju 88 C-6 of Ofw. Bindzus.	10 Kms. north-west of Lorient airfield.
	Ogefr. Heinz Barth	7	Bf	K				Lorient airfield.
	Ogefr. Claus Müller	7	Bb	K				
28-11-43	Uffz. Hermann Firnrohr	4		K			Aircraft crashed.	Mauritzen.
30-11-43	Uffz. Hermann Fischer	2	P	M	Ju 88 C-6	100%	Missing following combat with Sunderland.	
	Ogefr. Karl Speckin	2	Bf	M				
	Gefr. Rudolf Martin	2	Bb	M				
01-12-43	Lt. Gerhard Neumann	2	P	M	Ju 88 C-6	100%	Missing following combat with Mosquitos.	
	Ogefr. Ernst Feuerberg	2	Bf	M				
	Uffz. Wilhelm Meinz	2	Bb	M				
01-12-43	Ogefr. Max Vetter	2	P	M	Ju 88 C-6	100%	Missing following combat with Mosquitos.	
	Gefr. Wilfried Langhoff	2	Bf	M				
	Uffz. Helmut Rauer	2	Bb	M				
01-12-43	Fw. Walter Stohl	2	P	K	Ju 88 C-6	100%	Shot down in combat with four-engined bombers.	Pesch/Eifel.
	Uffz. Rudolf Hadatscheck	2	Bf	K				
	Uffz. Hermann Pflüger	2	Bb	K	750413			
01-12-43	Uffz. Anton Meierl	7	P	M	Ju 88 C-6	100%	Missing following combat with Mosquitos.	
	Uffz. Hans-Ullrich Gruntz	7	Bf	M	2N+SL			
	Fw. Herbert Nepomucky	7	Bb	M	750592			
12-12-43	Oblt. Hermann Horstmann (Staffelkapitän)	1	P	M	Ju 88 C-6	100%	Missing following combat with Beaufighters.	
	Fw. Georg Kunz	1	Bf	M				
	Fw. Rudolf Korczowy	1	Bb	M				
12-12-43	Lt. Friedrich Maeder	1	P	M	Ju 88 C-6	100%	Missing following combat with Beaufighters.	
	Uffz. Werner Ess	1	Bf	M				
	Ogefr. Herbert Baumert	1	Bb	M				
12-12-43	Uffz. Hans Frank	1	P	M	Ju 88 C-6	100%	Missing following combat with Beaufighters.	
	Gefr. Werner Göbler	1	Bf	M				
	Uffz. Adolf Wirth	1	Bb	M				
07-01-44	Uffz. Heinz Kohlhoff	4	P	K	Bf 110 G-2	100%	Shot down on combat mission.	Marchtrenk, near Wels.
	Uffz. Rolf Drews	4	Bf	K	2N+OM 120072			
07-01-44	Fw. Johann Pütz	7	P	M	Ju 88 C-6	100%	Missing after combat with 5 Mosquitos.	
	Uffz. Kurt Utlaut	7	Bf	M				
	Uffz. Josef Pittner	7	Bb	M	750388			
21-01-44	Ofw. Theodor Schweflinghaus	4	P	K	Bf 110 G-2	100%	Crashed on non-combat flight.	Oberweitersdorf, near
	Uffz. Heinrich Wetzel	4	Bf	K	2N+DP			Gallneukirchen.
	(4th Staffel crew flying a 6th Staffel aircraft)				6285			
01-02-44	Lt. Robert Baumann	7	P	PoW	Ju 88 C-6	100%	Did not return from combat mission.	
	Uffz. Herbert Jugnischke	7	Bf	M	2N+PK			
	Fw. Willi Held	7	Bb	M	360124			
01-02-44	Uffz. Helfried Schlegel	7	P	K	Ju 88 C-6	100%	Shot down on combat mission.	
	Uffz. Hermann Hegemann	7	Bf	K	2N+UR			
	Gefr. Franz Mroz	7	Bb	K	360079			
11-02-44	Lt. Herbert Jarmer	10	P	K	Fw190		Crashed after being hit by Flak.	8 Kms. north of Cap du Raz.
14-02-44	Oblt. Kurt Necesany	Gesch. Stab	P	M	Ju 88 C-6	100%	Did not return from combat mission.	
	Fw. Lothar Clemens	Gesch. Stab	Bf	M				
	Fw. Werner Rüger		Bb	M	750967			
14-02-44	Lt. Heinz Bickler	10	P	M	Fw190	100%	Missing on non-combat bombing practise flight.	2 Kms. south of Morgat,
22-02-44	Ofw. Franz Meissl	6	P	W	Bf 110 G-2 2N+FP 420009	100%	Shot down on combat mission.	East of Lichtenstein.
22-02-44	Uffz. Heinz Schlenkert	6	P	K	Bf 110 G-2 2N+GP 6417	100%	Shot down on combat mission.	Lichtenstein.
23-02-44	Uffz. Karl Scherz	4		W			Wounded on combat mission.	Gmunden.
23-02-44	Uffz. Rudolf Hiltner	5	P	K	Bf 110 G-2	100%	Shot down on combat mission.	Haag,10 Kms. south-
	Uffz. Hans Stöppler	5	Bf	K	2N+LN 6383			west of St. Valentin.

Date	Name of crew and rank	Staffel	Status	Fate	Aircraft code & W.Nr.	Damage state	Reason for casualty	Place
23-02-44	Uffz. Johann Rücker	6	P	K	Bf 110 G-2	100%	Shot down on combat mission.	8 Kms. south-west of
	Uffz. Karl Henze	6	Bf	K	2N+MP			Wels airfield.
					120171			
26-02-44	Fw. Heinz Baldeweg	3	P		Ju 88 C-6	100%	Aircraft lost on combat mission. Pilot safe.	
	Ogefr. Georg Blach	3	Bf	M	2N+PL			
	Fw. Wilhelm Buxbaum	3	Bb	M	750941			
07-03-44	Fw. Heinz Döhler	3	P	K	Ju 88 C-6	100%	Crashed on non-combat night flight.	6 Kms. south
	Uffz. Ernst Bongers	3	Bf	K			of Toulouse.	
	Uffz. Friedrich Gargulak	3	Bb	K	750894			
08-03-44	Oblt. Edgar Podzimek	1	P	M	Ju 88 C-6	100%	Escort to bomber unit. Shot down by British night-fighter.	
	Uffz. Paul Mohwinkel	1	Bf	M				
	Uffz. Hans Becker	1	Bb	M	750469			
08-03-44	Fw. Wilhelm Zimmer	2	P	M	Ju 88 C-6	100%	Escort to bomber unit. Missing after combat with	
	Uffz. Nikolaus Winter	2	Bf	M			Beaufighter.	
	Uffz. Artur Sieger	2	Bb	M	750893			
08-03-44	Uffz. Gerd Rauschke	2	P	K	Ju 88 C-6	100%	Escort to bomber unit. Shot down by Beaufighter.	
	Uffz. Heinrich Roensch	2	Bf	K				
	Uffz. Otto Hillenbrand	2	Bb	K	750709			
10-03-44	Obstlt. Lothar von Janson	Gesch. Stab	P	K	Ju 88 C-6	100%	Did not return from combat mission.	
	Uffz. Hans Schwarzrock	Gesch. Stab	Bf	M				
	Uffz. Heinz Scholdei	Gesch. Stab	Bb	M	750965			
10-03-44	Fw. Karl Bauer	7	P	K	Ju 88 C-6	100%	Shot down by British fighter.	
	Fw. Josef Mrechen	7	Bf	K				
	Uffz. Karl-Heinz Tomke	7	Bb	K				
11-03-44	Fw. Erich Hildebrandt	5	P	K	Bf 110 G-2	100%	Shot down on combat mission.	5 Kms. south-east of
	Uffz. Bernhard Rott	5	Bf	W	2N+CN			Wiener-Neustadt.
					120005			
13-03-44	Uffz. Herbert Altenhöner	3	P	K	Ju 88 C-6	100%	Crashed on non-combat night practise flight.	11Kms. south-east of
	Uffz. Helmut Kommar	3	Bf	K				Mont de Marsan.
	Uffz. Helmut Staas	3	Bb	K	360411			
13-03-44	Ogefr. Heinz Gehre	3	P	W	Ju 88 C-6	100%	Crashed on non-combat night practise flight	15 Kms. east of Mont
	Uffz. Eberhard Mölder	3	Bf	W				de Marsan.
	Gefr. Hermann Budde	3	Bb	W	750955			
23-03-44	Uffz. Rolf Leonhardt	2	P	K	Ju 88 C-6	100%	Crashed on non-combat flight.	28 Kms. east-north-east
	Uffz. Erich Haas	2	Bf	K				of Vannes.
	Uffz. Karl-Heinz Ewert	2	Bb	K	750719			
02-04-44	Uffz. Otto Schiller	4	P	K	Bf 110 G-2	100%	Did not return from combat mission.	Reichramin, south-
	Uffz. Karl Labecki	4	Bf	K	2N+PM			south-west of Steyr.
					150128			
02-04-44	Ofw. Alois Sonntag	5	P	K	Bf 110 G-2	100%	Shot down on combat mission.	Aigen airfield.
	Uffz. Erwin Kunze	5	Bf	W	2N+DN			
					150124			
02-04-44	Fhr. Fritz Walter	6	P	M	Bf 110 G-2	100%	Shot down on combat mission.	South of Steyr.
	Uffz. Christian Rodaro	6	Bf	M	2N+BP			
					6292			
02-04-44	Uffz. Peter Schölz	6	P	K	Bf 110 G-2	100%	Shot down on combat mission.	Wels airfield.
	Uffz. Rudolf Ullwer	6	Bf	K	2N+GP			
					5224			
05-04-44	Uffz. Hans Reichelmann	2	P	W	Ju 88 C-6		Rolled into bomb crater on return from combat	Vannes airfield.
	Ogefr. Hermann Weissbrod	2	Bf	W	2N+FK		mission and overturned.	
	Gefr. Edwin Hess	2	Bb	W	750411			
11-04-44	Hptm. Günther Moltrecht	1	P	K	Ju 88 R-2	100%	Missing following combat with Mosquitos.	
	(Staffelkapitän)							
	Uffz. Günther Dietermann	1	Bf	M	751043			
	Uffz. Hans Grötzinger	1	Bb	M				
11-04-44	Uffz. Hermann Forell	1	P	K	Ju 88 R-2	100%	Missing following combat with Mosquitos.	
	Ogefr. Wilhelm Beyer	1	Bf	K				
	Uffz. Hubert Kuhnert	1	Bb	K	750953			
11-04-44	Uffz. Josef Horvath	1	P	K	Ju 88 R-2	100%	Crashed into the sea following combat with Mosquitos.	
	Uffz. Paul Ullmann	1	Bf	W				
	Uffz. Werner Herrmann	1	Bb	W	751046			
11-04-44	Lt. Helmut Messerschmidt	2	P	M	Ju 88 C-6	100%	Missing following combat with Mosquitos.	
	Uffz. Hans Schüssler	2	Bf	M				
	Uffz. Rolf Stumpf	2	Bb	M	750891			
11-04-44	Uffz. Hans Reichelmann	2	P	M	Ju 88 C-6	100%	Crashed into the sea on combat mission.	
	Ogefr. Hermann Weissbrod	2	Bf	M				
	Ofw. Willy Boldt	2	Bb	M	750404			
11-04-44	Uffz. Gerhard Fritz	2	P	K	Ju 88 C-6	100%	Missing following combat mission.	
	Gefr. Hans Namhoff	1	Bf	W	720105			
11-04-44	Uffz. Fritz Sprang	3	P	W	Ju 88 C-6	100%	Crashed into the sea following combat with Mosquitos.	
	Uffz. Alfons Hiesinger	3	Bf	W	750961			
	Uffz. Wilhelm Lengfeld	3	Bb	M				
11-04-44	Lt. Klaus Uhsemann	9	P	K		100%	Crashed on non-combat flight. Both died on 12/4/44.	Saintes, 5 Kms. north-
	Ogefr. Heinrich Barnasch	9	Grdcrw	K				west of Saujon.
12-04-44	Fw. Herbert Oerzmann	4	P	K	Bf 110 G-2		Pilot killed on combat mission. Fate of Bordfunker	20 Kms. south-west of
					2N+KM		not known.	Wiener-Neustadt.
					120045			
12-04-44	Uffz. Walter Herkner	4	P	K	Bf 110 G-2	100%	Shot down on combat mission.	Alkersdorf, north-west of
	Fw. Franz Hummel	4	Bf	K	2N+GM			Wiener-Neustadt.
					6402			

Date	Name of crew and rank	Staffel	Status	Fate	Aircraft code & W.Nr.	Damage state	Reason for casualty	Place
12-04-44	Fw. Bernhardt Grundt	5	P	K	Bf 110 G-2 2N+MP 420027		Killed on combat mission.	15 Kms. north-east of Wiener-Neustadt.
12-04-44	Uffz. Eugen Dörr	5	P	K	Bf 110 G-2	100%	Shot down on combat mission.	Gols, near Parndorf.
	Uffz. Karl Erhart	5	Bf	W	2N+EN 5233			
12-04-44	Uffz. Hans Dobbertin	6	Bf	K	Bf 110 G-2 2N+AP 6129		Killed on combat mission.	South-west of Wiener-Neustadt.
13-04-44	Lt. Wilhelm Meilinger	4	P	K	Bf 110 G-2 2N+HM 6397	100%	Killed on combat mission.	7 Kms. south-east of Preßburg.
20-04-44	Lt. Josef Schwarz	3	P	M	Ju 88 C-6	100%	Escort for bomber unit - did not return from combat mission.	
	Uffz. Günther Brömel	3	Bf	M				
	Uffz. Helmut Schulte	3	Bb	M	750950			
20-04-44	Oblt. Martin Reuter (Staffelkapitän)	7	P	M	Ju 88 C-6	100%	Did not return from combat mission.	
	Uffz. Friedrich Blumenröther	7	Bf	M	750420			
	Uffz. Heinz Müller	7	Bb	M				
20-04-44	Uffz. Walter Kelle	7	P	M	Ju 88 C-6	100%	Did not return from combat mission.	
	Uffz. Kurt Berns	7	Bf	M				
	Uffz. Stefan Goos	7	Bb	M	750369			
20-04-44	Uffz. Horst Besdziek	7	P	M	Ju 88 C-6	100%	Did not return from combat mission.	
	Uffz. Erwin Bücken	7	Bf	M				
	Gefr. Gerhard Körner	7	Bb	M	360361			
24-04-44	Lt. Gerhard Diebel	6	P	K	Bf 110 G-2	100%	Non-combat flying accident.	Plattensee, Hungary.
	Uffz. Herbert Stille	6	Bf	K	2N+MP			
	Ogefr. Fritz Voigt	6	Grdcrw	K	5249			
02-05-44	Lt. Erich Angermayr	Erg. Zer. St. ZG 1	P	K	Ju 88 C-6	100%	Non-combat flying accident.	South-east of Windsheim.
	Gefr. Eduard Fetterroll		Bf	K				
	Gefr. Kurt Hermes		Bb	K	570595			
06-05-44	Uffz. Karl-Heinz Nickisch	4	P	M	Bf 110 G-2	100%	Did not return from combat mission.	Black Sea.
	Ogefr. Edmund Reinbacher	4	Bf	M	2N+KM 420117			
06-05-44	Lt. Helmut Ulke	5	P	M	Bf 110 G-2	100%	Did not return from combat mission.	Black Sea.
	Uffz. Otto Teitge	5	Bf	M	2N+IN 420003			
06-05-44	Uffz. Gerhard Fritsch	6	Bf	W	Bf 110 G-2 2N+EM 5408	25%	Bordfunker wounded on combat mission.	Over the Black Sea.
11-05-44	Uffz. Heinrich Lang	8	P		Ju 88 C-6	100%	Aircraft did not return from combat mission.	Mediterranean Sea.
	Ogefr. Werner Drewes	8	Bf	M			Uffz. Lang rescued and returned to unit.	
	Gefr. Hubert Licht	8	Bb	M				
20-05-44	Lt. Franz von Sprinzenstein	1	P	W	Ju 88 C-6	70%	Crash-landed upon return from combat mission.	Salon.
	Uffz. Paul Ullmann	1	Bb	W	750998			
24-05-44	Uffz. Horst Hermann	6	P	W	Bf 110 G-2 2N+JP 130075	100%	Written off following combat.	Hörsching airfield.
25-05-44	Ofw Heinrich Döscher	4	P	W	Bf 110 G-2		Crashed into another Bf 110 on take-off.	Wels airfield.
	Fw. Kurt Steiner	4	Bf	W	2N+GM 5405			
29-05-44	Ofw. Willhelm Schneider	4	P	K	Bf 110 G-2	100%	Shot down on combat mission.	Mödling, near Vienna.
	Uffz. Hermann Langenberg	4	Bf	K	2N+VM 410095			
29-05-44	Oblt. Fritz-Jochen Achenbach	5	P	K	Bf 110 G-2	100%	Shot down on combat mission.	Gutenstein.
	Uffz. Eugen Bees	5	Bf	K	2N+NN 5410			
29-05-44	Obfhr. Heinz Münker *(5th Staffel crew flying a 4th Staffel aircraft)*	5	P	K	Bf 110 G-2 2N+BM 170066		Casualty as a result of combat mission.	6 Kms. east of Isper.
29-05-44	Obfhr. Ruland Zahn	5	P	K	Bf 110 G-2 2N+FN 120173		Casualty as a result of combat mission.	Böheimkirchen, south-east of St. Polten.
29-05-44	Ofw. Herbert Stenger	5	P	K	Bf 110 G-2	100%	Shot down on combat mission.	Pottenstein.
	Uffz. Karl-Heinz Thümmel	5	Bf	K	2N+LN 120022			
29-05-44	Fw. Kurt Fischer	5	P	W	Bf 110 G-2		Casualties as a result of combat mission.	Schwarzau.
	Ogefr. Gerhard Wilcke	5	Bf	W	2N+RN 5262			
29-05-44	Uffz. Christian Böhme	5	P	K	Bf 110 G-2		Casualties as a result of combat mission.	Muggendorf.
	Uffz. Heinz Robakowski	5	Bf	W	2N+TN 5512			
29-05-44	Uffz. Heinrich Becker	5	Bf	W	Bf 110 G-2 2N+GN 5133		Bordfunker wounded on combat mission.	Laxenburg.
29-05-44	Oblt. Herbert Pelz	6	P	K	Bf 110 G-2	100%	Shot down on combat mission.	Gainfarn, near Bad Vöslau.
	Uffz. Richard Gerlach	6	Bf	K	2N+GP 130088			

Date	Name of crew and rank	Staffel	Status	Fate	Aircraft code & W.Nr.	Damage state	Reason for casualty	Place
29-05-44	Lt. Klaus Tillmann	6	P	K	Bf 110 G-2	100%	Shot down on combat mission.	Kleinzell.
	Uffz. Joachim Wienke	6	Bf	M	2N+BP			
					5616			
29-05-44	Lt. Siegward Winterhoff	6	P	W	Bf 110 G-2		Casualties as a result of combat mission.	
	Uffz. Gerhard Podschus	6	Bf	W	2N+SP			
					210094			
29-05-44	Fw. Hans Volkern	6	P	K	Bf 110 G-2	100%	Shot down on combat mission.	Berg Schöckel, north
	Uffz. Georg Kuschel	6	Bf	K	2N+TP			of Graz.
					6427			
29-05-44	Fw. Gotthard Wagner	6	P	K	Bf 110 G-2		Casualties as a result of combat mission.	Baden, near Vienna.
	Uffz. Hellmut Schranz	6	Bf	W	2N+PP			
					150108			
29-05-44	Uffz. Adolf Schwenk	6	P	K	Bf 110 G-2	100%	Shot down on combat mission.	Kleinzell.
	Uffz. Heinz Bayer	6	Bf	K	2N+OP			
					190098			
06-06-44	Uffz. Erich Keller	2	P	W	Ju 88 C-6	10%	Casualties as a result of combat mission.	Caen.
	Uffz. Othmar Kraml	2	Bf	W				
	Gefr. Fritz Sandermeier	2	Bb	W				
06-06-44	Uffz. Kurt Schwatz	2	P	M	Ju 88 C-6	100%	Did not return from combat mission.	North of Caen.
	Fw. Wilhelm Starkert	2	Bf	M	750924			
	Uffz. Karl Schmidt	2	Bb	M				
06-06-44	Uffz. Walter Herrmann	2	P	M	Ju 88 C-6	100%	Did not return from combat mission.	North of Caen.
	Gefr. Lothar Rams	2	Bf	K	750942			
	Gefr. Manfred Unger	2	Bb	M				
07-06-44	Uffz. Günther Theiss	1	P	W	Ju 88 C-6		Casualties as a result of combat with allied fighters.	Caen.
	Fw. Egon Purwin	3	Bf	K	750102			
	Ofw. Rudi Dobslaff	3	Bb	W				
07-06-44	Fw. Edmund Freiwald	2	P	M	Ju 88 C-6	100%	Did not return from combat mission.	North-west of Caen.
	Fw. Rudolf Gebicke	2	Bf	PoW				
	Uffz. Eugen Luttenberger	2	Bb	M	750104			
07-06-44	Uffz. Hans Roeder	2	P	M	Ju 88 C-6	100%	Did not return from combat mission.	North of Caen.
	Uffz. Heinrich Heymann	2	Bf	PoW	750401			
	Gefr. Lothar Schirmacher	2	Bb	M				
07-06-44	Ofw. Dietrich Wolf	2	P	K	Ju 88 C-6	90%	Casualty as a result of combat mission.	North-west of Caen.
					750374			
07-06-44	Uffz. Kurt Strobel	3	P	M	Ju 88 C-6	100%	Missing following combat with British fighters.	North of Caen.
	Uffz. Walter Schneider	3	Bf	M	2N+FK			
	Gefr. Erich Dressler	3	Bb	M	750411			
07-06-44	Lt. Kurt Löw	7	P	M	Ju 88 C-6	100%	Did not return from combat mission.	
	Uffz. Heinrich Seifert	7	Bf	M	360431			
	Fhj-Fw. Gerhard Haberger	Stab, III. Gruppe	Bb	M				
07-06-44	Fw. Josef Hollerith	7	P	M	Ju 88 C-6	100%	Did not return from combat mission.	
	Uffz. Johann Lechner	7	Bf	M	750699			
	Ogefr. Helmut Rieger	7	Bb	M				
07-06-44	Lt. Ulrich Hanshen	III. Gruppe	P	M	Ju 88 C-6	100%	Did not return from combat mission.	
	Ofw. Werner Herrmann	III. Gruppe	Bf	M	750899			
	Ofw. Fritz Quapp	III. Gruppe	Bb	M				
09-06-44	Lt. Knud Gmelin	1	P	K	Ju 88 C-6	100%	Shot down by Flak.	Caen.
	Uffz. Gerhard Zimmermann	1	Bf	W	750897			
	Uffz. Wilhelm Dunker	1	Bb	W				
09-06-44	Uffz. Ludwig Dietler	2	Bf	M	Ju 88 C-6		Bordfunker missing following combat mission.	
					750892			
09-06-44	Fw. Fritz Hänel	Erg. St. ZG 1	P	K			Casualties as a result of combat mission.	
	Uffz. Karl Obermeyer	Erg. St. ZG 1	Bf	K				
10-06-44	Uffz. Erich Engeln	7	P	M	Ju 88 C-6	100%	Did not return from combat mission.	
	Uffz. Otto Sommer	7	Bf	K	750335			
	Flgr. Hans Cox	7	Bb	PoW				
10-06-44	Uffz. Xavier Schmeidberger	9	P	K	Ju 88 C-6	100%	Did not return from combat mission.	
	Uffz. Heinz Masmeier	9	Bf	K	360316			
	Gefr. Erwin Lamla	9	Bb	K				
13-06-44	Oblt. Rolf Witthoff	4	P	K	Bf 110 G-2	100%	Shot down on combat mission.	Hohenkammern, near
	Uffz. Richard Foetze	4	Bf	K	2N+KM			Freysing.
					120059			
15-06-44	Fhj.-Uffz. Karl Ronde	4	P	K	Bf 110 G-2		Right engine failed on non-combat flight.	Großraming, south-west
					2N+MM			of Steyr.
					6288			
26-06-44	Lt. Kurt Strölin	6	P	K	Bf 110 G-2		Casualties as a result of combat mission.	Malacky, south-east of
	Uffz. Kurt Matz	6	Bf	K	2N+GP			Preßburg.
					170077			
26-06-44	Fw. Erich Stiemke	6	P	K	Bf 110 G-2	100%	Shot down on combat mission.	Schweinsbach, near
	Uffz. Kurt Immisch	6	Bf	K	2N+JP			Malacky.
					130097			
26-06-44	Fhr. Hugo Feindt	6	P	W	Bf 110 G-2	100%	Shot down on combat mission.	Malacky, south-east of
	Ogefr. Helmut Döpke	6	Bf	K	2N+AP			Preßburg.
					130083			
26-06-44	Ogefr. Hermann Boek	6	Bf	K	Bf 110 G-2	30%	Casualty as a result of combat mission.	Preßburg airfield.
					2N+PP			
					130061			

Date	Name of crew and rank	Staffel	Status	Fate	Aircraft code & W.Nr.	Damage state	Reason for casualty	Place
27-06-44	Lt. Werner Witter Uffz. Johannes Guse	4 4	P Bf	W W	Bf 110 G-2 2N+AM 6401		Casualties as a result of combat mission.	Budapest.
27-06-44	Lt. Wilhelm Stieghan Fw. Werner Mobius	4 4	P Bf	K K	Bf 110 G-2 2N+EM 5408	100%	Shot down on combat mission.	21Kms. north-west of Budapest.
27-06-44	Hptm. Rudi Wangner	5	P	K	Bf 110 G-2 2N+KN 120049		Casualty as a result of combat mission.	South of Budapest.
27-06-44	Uffz. Artur Stölzel Fhr. Helmut Hils	5 5	P Bf	K K	Bf 110 G-2 2N+CN 6925	100%	Shot down on combat mission.	Budapest.
27-06-44	Ofw. Siegfried Schuhbauer Uffz. Herbert Reim	5 5	P Bf	K W	Bf 110 G-2 2N+EN 150127		Casualties as a result of combat mission.	20 Kms. north of Budapest.
27-06-44	Fw. Kurt Fischer Ogefr. Gerhard Wilcke	5 5	P Bf	K W	Bf 110 G-2 2N+RN 6128		Casualties as a result of combat mission.	100 Kms. north of Budapest.
27-06-44	Ofw. Heinrich Börger Fw. Heinrich Bomer	6 6	P Bf	W K	Bf 110 G-2 2N+CP 130071		Casualties as a result of combat mission.	Leva.
27-06-44	Ofhr. Joachim Pfüller Uffz. Konrad Dreifke	6 6	P Bf	W W	Bf 110 G-2 2N+QP 130087		Casualties as a result of combat mission.	Pomatz,18 Kms. north-west of Budapest.
28-06-44	Flgr. Gerhard Schmidt Uffz. Anton Steinmetz	6 6	P Bf	K K	Bf 110 G-2 2N+HP 420129	100%	Crashed on combat mission.	Picheln, near Wels.
28-06-44	Uffz. Werner Horst Migge Ogefr. Horst Michael Ogefr. Hans Joachim Köhler	9 9 9	P Bf Bb	K M K	Ju 88 C-6 750898	100%	Did not return from combat mission.	2 Kms. east of Danvey, near Chateaudun.
02-07-44	Uffz. Horst Schumann Uffz. Heinz Mayer	5 5	P Bf	K K	Bf 110 G-2 2N+UN 6300	100%	Did not return from combat mission.	Budapest.
03-07-44	Uffz. Willi Weber	Erg. St. ZG 1	P	K	Bücker131A 1E+10D 4420	100%	Crashed on non-combat flight.	14 Kms. north-north-west of Ansbach.
03-07-44	Uffz. Karl Brandt	Erg. St. ZG 1	P	K	Bücker131A 1E+12D 317	100%	Crashed on non-combat flight.	14 Kms. north-north-west of Ansbach.

Appendix 2
Reports

II./Zerstörergeschwader 1 Command Post, 5.2.1942

Copy!

Tamm, Feldw. 4.2.42
II./Z.G. 1

Report

I flew as Number 3 in the Rotte of Hauptmann Kaldrack in the attack on Basary airfield (17683) on 3.2.42. On the airfield an R-5 had force-landed and had been set on fire with Hptm. Kaldrack's second attack. Hptm. Kaldrack then pulled away and Oblt. Ortmann followed closely. I followed some way behind. Suddenly my Bordfunker reported: Fighters behind! I looked around, saw the machine about 100 m to the side behind me and identified it as a I-18. Thereupon I immediately turned. After three 360º turns the aircraft went into a half right turn. I called over the radio: I am in combat with an I-18! As a result both aircraft immediately arrived. Hptm. Kaldrack curved into the I-18 and Oblt. Ortmann was close behind him. The I-18 circled ever tighter. As Hptm. Kaldrack positioned himself behind it, I saw the machine of Oblt. Ortmann crash into the machine of Hptm Kaldrack around the Bordfunker's position. Then I only saw burning and other pieces of both machines fly all around. I did not see any parachutes open. I could not see anything further, as I got myself into a favourable position behind the I-18, shot it down, and in turn was attacked from behind by an I-18 and in the ensuing combat left the crash area.

gez. Tamm

F. d. R. d. A.

Certified a true copy

gez. Gluth

Oberleutnant and Adjutant

•••••

Copy!

Klebert, 20.2.42
Obfeldw., 5./Z.G. 1

Report

On 11.2.42 I took off as wingman to Oblt. v. Lölhöffel. The mission order was: "Low-level attack in the area Demidow - Welish - Surash." After several attacks in the area south-east of Demidow we flew course 30º and reached the Demidow - Welish road. Over Pjetschenki I saw more LKW, which were covered in snow on the road. I informed Oblt. v. Lölhöffel over the radio, whereupon we flew over the LKW, as a result of which we established that they were not serviceable. Following that Oblt. v. Lölhöffel pulled up and headed in the direction of Welish. As I pulled up, my left motor suddenly failed, so I notified the lead machine that, as a result of a seized left engine, I was returning home, for which I received acknowledgement. I then flew in the direction of the airfield, while Oblt. v. Lölhöffel continued on the earlier course (Welish).

A search undertaken on 13.2.42 by a Rotte, Oblt. Heilmeyer and myself, remained unsuccessful.

gez. Klebert

F.d.R.d.A.

Oberleutnant and Adjutant

•••••

Schummer, Leutnant 13.6.42
6. Zerstörergeschwader 1

Report

On 11.6.42 I flew an armed reconnaissance mission as Nr. 3 in the Schwarm of Oblt. Heilmayer in the area of Woltschansk - Belyj Kolodos and south-east thereof. The Schwarm consisted of Oblt. Heilmayer as Schwarm Leader, Uffz. Pfeiffer Nr. 2 and Uffz. Fritzer as Nr. 4. Take off: 08.30 hours. After successful reconnaissance in the allotted area, the Schwarm circled several times above and below the clouds, and finally at around 09.40 hours, probably at grid reference 2724, came out of the clouds at a height of 1000 meters on a southerly course. At this point Uffz. Pfeiffer was hit by Flak and turned right to fly home. Oblt. Heilmayer flew eastwards at a height of 900 meters. As a result Oblt. Heilmayer, probably at grid reference 2862, received 2 hits from light Flak, resulting in a stab of flame being seen in the cockpit. Soon after, one of the crew bailed out, probably the Funker Uffz. Hörger. A parachute opened immediately. The machine flew on, went into a glide in a left turn, and appeared to be preparing for a belly landing. I then saw how the machine suddenly tipped forward and from 2-300 meters height, probably at grid reference 2847, crashed into the forest. The machine was destroyed by fire.

Because of the last machine remaining behind, my attention was almost totally diverted from getting the true bearings. I cannot therefore identify the location with certainty.

•••••

Böck, Franz, Uffz. 25.4.43
6. /II. /ZG 1

<u>Witness Report</u>

On 17.4.43 I flew with my Bordfunker, Uffz. Henry Ahrens, on escort duty for ships from Sicily to Tunis. Near Cap Bone our formation was attacked by about 25 Spitfires. In the course of combat I received hits in both engines and had to land on the sea. Prior to the emergency landing I was in contact with my Bordfunker through "Ei-V". Before the aircraft settled on the sea I no longer heard answers. As we were still being hit by attacking Spitfires, it was assumed that Uffz. Ahrens was wounded. I managed to free myself from the aircraft at the last moment, as it sank immediately. After swimming around the area for ten minutes until I was rescued by an Italian destroyer, I did not see Uffz. Ahrens again.

•••••

Schwidtal, Leutnant 14.6.43
6. /Zerstörergeschwader 1

<u>Witness Report</u>

On 1.5.43 I had the assignment, as Rotte Leader in a formation which was led by Oblt. Eiffländer, to ferry air material from Trapani to Tunis. Near Cap Bone we were attacked by superior numbers of English fighters. In the course of combat our formation was split up. After 10 minutes of combat I was able to disengage with my Rottenflieger, Lt. Meyer, S9+IP, who had flown behind me for the whole of the combat, and set course North. After 5 minutes flying I turned towards home, but I saw that Lt. Meyer continued to fly north. I turned towards him, as I was already 1 Km. distant from him, and saw at that moment his machine hit the sea, and after an explosion sink immediately. After flying twice over the crash site, which still had burning fuel on the waves, I could not see the Bf 110 or the crew.

•••••

Hartmann Willi Oberleutnant 23.7.43
6./II./Zerstörergeschwader 1

Report on the mission on 19.7.43 05:30 Hours

On 19.7.43, 05:30 hours, I took off from Montecorvino (Italy) as Nr. 4 with the mission order: Bombing attack on enemy artillery positions south-west of Catania.

After we had dropped our bombs we flew at low level in the direction of Catania and from there in a fairly tight formation 3-5 Km. from the coast over the sea in the direction of Messina-Montecorvino. We flew in Schwarm formation echelon right at about 500 m. height. I was somewhat adrift, while the first three aircraft flew in tight formation.

Over Taomina, I noticed tracer fire pass by Nr. 2. I immediately gave full throttle, tipped my aircraft over the left wing and saw below me to the left about 50 m. away a Spitfire. As the Spitfire also used full throttle and hung beneath me, I was unable to fire at him. Behind me sat two enemy fighters, of which my Funker immediately shot down the first one. I turned left towards our aircraft, in order to join up with the formation again. At the same time I saw our Nr. 2 turn to the right and by so doing ram Nr. 3. Aircraft. Nr. 2 burst into flames immediately with large black smoke, while the left wing of Nr. 3 broke off. I saw Nr. 3 dive steeply and crash. Due to being in combat I could not make any other observations. I also could not see anybody attempting to save themselves by taking to their parachute.

•••••

<u>Copy.</u>

Grundt, Bernhardt 21.7.43
Feldw. 5./Z.G. 1

Report on the mission on
19.7.43 05:30 Hours

On 19.7.1943 at 0530 hours I took off with my Bordfunker, Uffz. Kurt Geyer, from Montecorvino (Italy) with the mission order: Bombing attack on enemy artillery positions south-west of Catania. I flew in S9+CN, W.Nr. 6229 as Nr. 3.

After we had dropped our bombs we flew at low level in the direction of Catania. From there in a tight formation 3-5 Km. from the coast over the sea in the direction of Messina-Montecorvino. 20 Kms. north of Taormina at 0730 hours we were attacked at a height of 600 m. by 4 Spitfires. The Schwarm Leader, Oberfeldw. Döscher, after giving the alarm, made an immediate left turn in order to form an Abwehrkreis. At this point I noticed that the aircraft S9+EM, in which pilot Uffz. Hillmann and Bordfunker Uffz. Jauernick were flying, already showed coolant flowing from the left engine. While we were forming the Abwehrkreis, Uffz. Hillmann suddenly made a sharp turn to the right. Because there were so many machines close by, it was not possible for my aircraft to avoid that of Uffz. Hillmann. As a result, my machine's left wing hit the fuselage of S9+EM. As the left wing of my machine broke off, I could see that Uffz. Hillmann flew on beneath me. My aircraft immediately turned over and plummeted. I gave my Bordfunker the order to bail out immediately. After not receiving any reply from my Bordfunker, I ejected the cockpit roof, freed myself, and leapt clear of the machine. I opened my parachute while I was in a horizontal position. As I hung on my parachute, I could see nearby my machine crash into the sea. I fell into the sea on my back and freed myself instantly from my parachute; immediately opened the air valve of my life jacket and came to the surface of the waves. I saw nothing more of my aircraft, also I could not establish the whereabouts of my Bordfunker.

As I was swimming in the water, I saw a Spitfire crash about 300-400 m. up a mountain slope and saw the pilot on the end of his parachute land nearby in the water. When I spotted 2 Me 110s flying over me, I fired one white flare from my signal pistol. After I got my dinghy ready and managed to climb into it, I noticed that because of the wind and sea current I was being driven out to sea; as a result I deployed the sea anchor. I then fired off several more emergency flares.

At around 1100 hours I was rescued by an Italian rowing boat. On the way back to land I saw a second dinghy. We headed for the dinghy and established that the occupant was English. After I had taken the Englishman prisoner and removed his firearm, he proved to be Sergeant Downing from London. We took the Englishman on board and reached land at about 1200 hours. I passed the prisoner over to Italian authorities in Teresa die Riva. I returned to Messina in a military vehicle, was ferried across, and headed back to my unit base, where I reported back on 20.7.43.

F.d.R.d.A. gez. Grundt.

.....

Kayl, 24.8.43
Oberleutnant, 5./ZG 1

Witness Report

of the crash of aircraft Bf 110 "S9+GN" W.Nr. 6406
Crew Uffz. Planer - Uffz. Hoffmann

On 21.8.43 at about 18.00 hours I took off with a Schwarm of Bf 110s on a free hunt over the Atlantic. At about 19.20 hours we sighted a Liberator at a height of about 400 m.. I attacked it from below left from the front and turned after the first attack beneath the aircraft to the left below in the direction of the enemy aircraft. Uffz. Planer flew with me as Nr. 2. Suddenly my Funker Feldw. Fuchs shouted: Uffz. Planer has crashed. I turned more and saw only a burning spot on the waves. I flew to the crash site but, aside from see burning wreckage, could not see that anyone had got out of the aircraft. The height at the moment of the crash was about 150 m.. It can be assumed with certainty that the crew of Uffz. Planer - Uffz. Hoffmann died the heroes death.

gez. Kayl
Oberleutnant

F. d. R. d. A.

Leutnant u.Adjutant

.....

Copy

Eye witness report on the crash of Bf 110, S9+EN,
Crew Lt. Bambauer - Uffz. Grotsch

We were involved in combat with 4 Mosquitos. During a turn following an attack I saw at the same height as me the machine of Leutnant Bambauer go into the sea at an angle of 30°. I could see the cockpit roof jettisoned, but did not see anyone get out of the machine. I could not see anything further happen, as I was again engaged in combat.

gez. Dörr , Uffz.

I, as Funker of Uffz. Dörr, saw the Machine at the same angle, saw that the Funker had jettisoned the cockpit roof and that there were red flames in the cabin, and saw further how the Pilot brought the machine into a horizontal position and sideslipped. The height at this point was about 50 meters. Then it disappeared from my sight. Of the crew, I saw no one bail out.

gez. Erhart , Uffz.

Note: the date of this loss was 11 September 1943.

.....

Copy
Ruland Zahn, Ofw. O.U., 28.9.43
5./Z.G. 1

Report on the death of
Feldw. Ernst Patzke

On the order to scramble on 24.9.43 to intercept an enemy bomber formation, I took off with my Bordfunker Ernst Patzke as Number 3 in the first Schwarm. We pulled ahead of the other Schwarms to intercept the enemy formation, and climbed and saw them with a strong escort of about 40 fighters, to the right above us. It was about 7 minutes after take-off when the enemy fighters saw us and dived on us from all sides. I was attacked from left and right at the same time by about 4 -6 Spitfires, turned left and with my first burst shot down a Spitfire in front of me, and then sought to shake off six Spitfires sitting behind me. My Bordfunker, Fw. Patzke, fired a few rounds, we received the first hits in the left motor, which caught fire immediately. From this moment on I no longer heard from my Bordfunker, and believed that he was badly wounded. Shortly afterwards I had to get out of the machine, which crashed and sank into the sea in grid reference 5971.

gez. Zahn

F.d.R.d.A.

Lt. u. Adjutant

Appendix 3
Flugbuch entries of Karl-Fritz Schröder

3. Staffel, Schnellkampfgeschwader 210 & Zerstörergeschwader 1

Karl-Fritz Schröder's Flugbuch entries record many of the major events in the history of the Wespengeschwader. Starting a week after the formation of Schnellkampfgeschwader 210, they chart the night missions against England in the spring of 1941, flying the Messerschmitt 210 with Erprobungsstaffel 210, and then the move to the Russian front for missions in 1942, where Schröder and his pilot Lußky were shot down by a Russian tank during a low level attack on 1st July 1942. Schröder survived being shot down a second time on the Russian front while flying with 13.(Z)/JG 5, spending several days behind Russian lines before regaining the German side.

Flight No.	Pilot	Crew	Type	Code	Type of Flight	Take-off place	Take-off day	Take-off time	Landing place	Landing day	Landing time	flight time	Kms.
99	Lußky Uffz.	Gefr. Schröder	Bf 110	S9+EL	Orientation flight	Merville	29.4.41		Merville	29.4.41	11.20	70	
100	Lußky	Schröder	Bf 110	S9+ML	Bombing practise	Merville	29.4.41	16.25	Merville	29.4.41	16.35	10	
101	Lußky	Schröder	Bf 110	S9+ML	Bombing practise	Merville	29.4.41	16.50	Merville	29.4.41	17.00	10	
102	Lußky	Schröder	Bf 110	S9+DL	Orientation flight	Merville	30.4.41	10.15	Merville	30.4.41	11.50	95	
103	Lußky	Schröder	Bf 110	S9+ML	Enemy flight - E	Merville	2.5.41	18.55	Merville	2.5.41	20.15	80	2
	Remarks: Armed reconnaissance over England. Cloudless near Great Yarmouth.												
104	Lußky	Schröder	Bf 110	S9+EL	UKW flight	Merville	3.5.41	0945	Merville	3.5.41	10.15	30	
105	Lußky	Schröder	Bf 110	S9+ML	Enemy flight - E	Merville	4.5.41	2230	Merville	4.5.41	0025	115	3
	Remarks: Attack on Ipswich. Lots of searchlights. Almost no Flak. Night flight. Bombs on Clacton.												
106	Lußky	Schröder	Bf 110	S9+ML	Enemy flight - E	Merville	5.5.41	2140	Merville	5.5.41	2325	105	4
	Remarks: Bombs on Clacton-on-Sea. Attack on Searchlight.												
107	Lußky	Schröder	Bf 110	S9+ML	Enemy flight - E	Merville	6.5.41	2123	Merville	6.5.41	2340	137	5
	Remarks: 1 hour low level flight over England. Flak! Target not found. Bombs on Clacton.												
108	Lußky	Schröder	Bf 110	S9+ML	Enemy flight - E	Merville	7.5.41	2128	Merville	7.5.41	2340	142	6
	Remarks: Coastal shipping attacked near Great Yarmouth. Hits in the wings and cockpit. Lußky wounded. Fighter! Got back on one engine. Lt. Mejer†												
109	Lußky	Schröder	Bf 110	S9+LL	Enemy flight - E	Merville	20.5.41	1755	Merville	1928,	93	7	
	Remarks: Armed reconnaissance near Great Yarmouth. Cloudless.												
110	Lußky	Schröder	Bf 110	S9+IL	Enemy flight - E	Merville	25.5.41	2055	Merville	25.5.41	2203	112	8
	Remarks: Armed reconnaissance. Sortie for blind-flying in the Thames estuary.												
111	Lußky	Schröder	Bf 110	S9+ML	Transfer flight	Merville	31.5.41	1635	Lippstadt	31.5.41	1800	85	
112	Disper† Lt.	Schröder	Bf 110	S9+ML	Practise flight	Lippstadt	5.5.41	0917	Lippstadt	5.5.41	1050	93	
113	Meyer-Erlach Lt.	Schröder	Bf 110	S9+LL	Transport flight	Sechtschinskaja	22.9.41	1355	Orscha	22.9.41	1505	70	
	Remarks: Russia!!!												
114	Meyer-Erlach	Schröder	Bf 210	S9+BL	Take-off practise	Landsberg	5.12.41	1030	Landsberg	5.12.41	1038	8	
115	Meyer-Erlach	Schröder	Bf 210	S9+BL	Take-off practise	Landsberg	5.12.41	1042	Landsberg	5.12.41	1049	7	
116	Meyer-Erlach	Schröder	Bf 210	S9+BL	Take-off practise	Landsberg	5.12.41	1053	Landsberg	5.12.41	1102	9	
117	Meyer-Erlach	Schröder	Bf 210	S9+BL	Take-off practise	Landsberg	5.12.41	1106	Landsberg	5.12.41	1112	6	
118	Meyer-Erlach	Schröder	Bf 210	S9+BL	Take-off practise	Landsberg	5.12.41	1116	Landsberg	5.12.41	1133	17	
119	Brandel Flg.	Schröder	Bf 108	BL+YZ	Transport flight	Landsberg	5.12.41	1510	München-Riem	5.12.41	1535	25	
120	Meyer-Erlach	Schröder	Bf 110	S9+BN	Transport flight	München-Riem	6.12.41	0910	Landsberg	6.12.41	0930	12	
121	Meyer-Erlach	Schröder	Bf 210	S9+CL	Practise flight	Landsberg	6.12.41	1410	Landsberg	6.12.41	1419	9	
122	Meyer-Erlach	Schröder	Bf 210	S9+BL	Practise flight	Landsberg	7.12.41	0904	Landsberg	7.12.41	0921	17	
123	Meyer-Erlach Oblt.	Schröder	Bf 210	S9+BL	Practise flight	Landsberg	7.12.41	0931	Landsberg	7.12.41	0943	12	
124	Meyer-Erlach	Schröder	Bf 210	S9+BL	Practise flight	Landsberg	7.12.41	0947	Landsberg	7.12.41	0955	8	
125	Meyer-Erlach	Schröder	Bf 210	S9+BL	Practise flight	Landsberg	7.12.41	1000	Landsberg	7.12.41	1008	8	
126	Meyer-Erlach	Schröder	Bf 210	S9+BL	Practise flight	Landsberg	7.12.41	1011	Landsberg	7.12.41	1020	9	
127	Meyer-Erlach	Schröder	Bf 210	S9+BL	Practise flight	Landsberg	8.12.41	1241	Landsberg	8.12.41	1306	25	
128	Meyer-Erlach	Schröder	Bf 210	S9+CL	Practise flight	Landsberg	8.12.41	1309	Landsberg	8.12.41	1323	14	
129	Meyer-Erlach	Schröder	Bf 210	S9+CL	Practise flight	Landsberg	8.12.41	1326	Landsberg	8.12.41	1334	8	
130	Meyer-Erlach	Schröder	Bf 210	S9+CL	Practise flight	Landsberg	8.12.41	1443	Landsberg	8.12.41	1537	54	
131	Meyer-Erlach	Schröder	Bf 210	S9+CH	Practise flight	Landsberg	8.12.41	1602	Landsberg	8.12.41	1610	8	
132	Meyer-Erlach	Schröder	Bf 210	S9+HL	Practise flight	Landsberg	8.12.41	1617	Landsberg	8.12.41	1621	4	
133	Meyer-Erlach	Schröder	Bf 210	S9+HL	Practise flight	Landsberg	8.12.41	1624	Landsberg	8.12.41	1632	8	
134	Meyer-Erlach	Schröder	Bf 210	S9+CL	Practise flight	Landsberg	9.12.41	1730	Landsberg	9.12.41	1740	10	
135	Meyer-Erlach	Schröder	Bf 210	S9+CL	Bombing practise	Landsberg	11.12.41	1134	Landsberg	11.12.41	1154	20	
136	Meyer-Erlach Uffz.	Schröder	Bf 210	S9+DL	Formation flight	Lechfeld	14.1.42	1614	Lechfeld	14.1.42	1701	47	
137	Meyer-Erlach	Schröder	Bf 210	S9+DL	Practise flight	Lechfeld	15.1.42	1410	Lechfeld	15.1.42	1430	20	
138	Meyer-Erlach	Schröder	Bf 210	S9+DL	Practise flight	Lechfeld	15.1.42	1445	Lechfeld	15.1.42	1525	40	
139	Meyer-Erlach	Schröder	Bf 210	S9+AL	Practise flight	Lechfeld	20.1.42	1447	Lechfeld	20.1.42	1508	21	
140	Meyer-Erlach	Schröder	Bf 210	S9+EL	Practise flight	Lechfeld	25.1.42	1007	Lechfeld	25.1.42	1015	8	
141	Meyer-Erlach	Schröder	Bf 210	S9+DL	Practise flight	Lechfeld	25.1.42	1507	Lechfeld	25.1.42	1517	10	
142	Meyer-Erlach	Schröder	Bf 210	S9+DL	Practise flight	Lechfeld	25.1.42	1520	Lechfeld	25.1.42	1530	10	
143	Meyer-Erlach	Schröder	Bf 210	S9+EL	Practise flight	Lechfeld	28.1.42	1025	Lechfeld	28.1.42	1059	34	
144	Meyer-Erlach	Schröder	Bf 210	S9+IH	Transfer flight	Lechfeld	2.3.42	1720	Tours	2.3.42	1935	130	
145	Schwab Lt.	Schröder	Bf 210	S9+IL	Airfield flight	Tours	3.3.42	1644	Tours	3.3.42	1657	13	
146	Schwab	Schröder	Bf 210	S9+IL	Airfield flight	Tours	3.3.42	1706	Tours	3.3.42	1712	12	
147	Schwab	Schröder	Bf 210	S9+IL	Practise flight	Tours	3.3.42	1718	Tours	3.3.42	1731	13	
148	Schwab	Schröder	Bf 210	S9+KL	Low level flight	Tours	8.3.42	1715	Tours	8.3.42	1740	25	
149	Schwab	Schröder	Bf 210	S9+IL	Formation flight	Tours	9.3.42	1657	Tours	9.3.42	1740	43	
	Remarks: Engine damage. Belly landing.												

Flight No.	Pilot	Crew	Type	Code	Type of Flight	Take-off place	Take-off day	Take-off time	Landing place	Landing day	Landing time	flight time	Kms.
150	Lußky Fw.	Schröder	W34	RC+CJ	Courier flight	Tours	1.4.42	1225	Flers	1.4.42	1355	90	
151	Lußky	Schröder	W34	RC+CJ	Courier flight	Flers, Norm.	1.4.42	1530	Tours	1.4.42	1708	98	
152	Boxhammer Oblt.	Schröder	Bf 110	S9+AL	Practise flight	Neubiberg	24.4.42	0934	Neubiberg	24.4.42	1040	54	
153	Boxhammer	Schröder	Bf 110	S9+AL	Bombing practise	Neubiberg	27.4.42	1416	Neubiberg	27.4.42	1531	75	
154	v. Rabenau Lt.	Schröder	Bf 110	S9+FL	Formation flight	Neubiberg	28.4.42	1423	Neubiberg	28.4.42	1500	37	
155	v. Rabenau	Schröder	Bf 110	S9+EL	Formation flight	Neubiberg	29.4.42	0930	Neubiberg	29.4.42	1010	40	
156	Boxhammer†	Schröder	Bf 110	S9+LL	Formation fllight	Neubiberg	14.5.42	0700	Lechfeld	14.5.42	0717	17	
157	Boxhammer	Schröder	Bf 210	GE+KU	Practise flight	Lechfeld	14.5.42	0925	Lechfeld	14.5.42	1131	126	
	Remarks: Goodbye 210!												
158	Boxhammer	Schröder	Bf 110	S9+LL	Transport flight	Lechfeld	14.5.42	1634	Neibiberg	14.5.42	1725	51	
160	v. Rabenau	Schröder	Bf 110	S9+RL	Transport flight	Neubiberg	29.5.42	0858	Krakau	29.5.42	1110	132	
	Remarks: Russia II.												
161	v. Rabenau	Schröder	Bf 110	S9+RL	Transfer flight	Krakau	29.5.42	1438	Proskurow	29.5.42	1630	128	
	Remarks: Bobby†, Box†												
162	v. Rabenau	Schröder	Bf 110	S9+RL	Transfer flight	Proskurow	30.5.42	0902	Uman	30.5.42	1002	60	
163	v. Rabenau	Schröder	Bf 110	S9+RL	Transfer flight	Uman	30.5.42	1405	Uman	30.5.42	1425	20	
164	v. Rabenau	Schröder	Bf 110	S9+RL	Transfer flight	Uman	31.5.42	1335	Charkow Süd	31.5.42	1520	105	
165	v. Rabenau	Schröder	Bf 110	S9+RL	Transfer flight	Charkow	31.5.42	1638	Bjelgorod	31.5.42	1658	20	
9 166	v. Rabenau	Schröder	Bf 110	S9+PL	Enemy flight	Bjelgorod	3.6.42	1452	Bjelgorod	3.6.42	1634	102	1R
	Remarks: Reconnaissance in Woltschansk area. Attack on troops.												
10 167	v. Rabenau	Schröder	Bf 110	S9+SL	Enemy flight	Bjelgorod III	10.6.42	0240	10 Km. south of Bjelgorod	10.6.42	0355	75	2R
	Remarks: Emergency landing in a corn field.												
11 168	Kötz Lt.	Schröder	Bf 110	S9+TL	Enemy flight	Bjelgorod	19.6.42	0445	Bjelgorod	19.6.42	0540	55	3R
	Remarks: Reconnaissance. Attack on field emplacements.												
12 169	Kötz Lt.	Schröder	Bf 110	S9+RL	Enemy flight	Bjelgorod	22.6.42	0250	Bjelgorod	22.6.42	0430	110	4R
	Remarks: Reconnaissance and attack in the Kapjans area.												
13 170	Kötz Lt.	Schröder	Bf 110	S9+KL	Enemy flight	Bjelgorod	24.6.42	0245	Bjelgorod	24.6.42	0325	40	5R
	Remarks: Attack on enemy emplacements in woods near Schenekino.												
14 171	Kötz Lt.	Schröder	Bf 110	S9+KL	Enemy flight	Bjelgorod	24.6.42	1250	Bjelgorod	24.6.42	1425	95	6R
	Remarks: Attack on troop concentrations in Ssenkowo.												
15 172	Kötz Lt.	Schröder	Bf 110	S9+IL	Enemy flight	Bjelgorod	28.6.42	0337	Bjelgorod	28.6.42	0512	99	7R
	Remarks: Attack on the railroad Belo-Kuraki.												
16 173	Kötz Lt.	Schröder	Bf 110	S9+IL	Enemy flight	Bjelgorod	30.6.42	0250	Bjelgorod	30.6.42	0425	95	8R
	Remarks: Attack on artillery emplacements.												
17 174	Kötz Lt.	Schröder	Bf 110	S9+IL	Enemy flight	Bjelgorod	30.6.42	0715	Bjelgorod	30.6.42	0805	50	9R
	Remarks: Attack on tanks and fortifications.												
18 175	Kötz Lt.	Schröder	Bf 110	S9+IL	Enemy flight	Bjelgorod	30.6.42	1215	Bjelgorod	30.6.42	1350	95	10R
	Remarks: Attack on armored vehicles and emplacements.												
19 176	Lußky Fw.	Schröder	Bf 110	S9+KL	Enemy flight	Bjelgorod	1.7.42	1215					11R
	Remarks: Bjelgo Shot down by a Russian tank and landed 500 m. behind the lines!												
20 177	Kötz Lt.	Schröder	Bf 110	S9+IL	Enemy flight	Bjelgorod	4.7.42	1310	Bjelgorod	4.7.42	1427	87	12R
	Remarks: Attack on troops in the Rassnoje area.												

Notes:

'E' denotes a mission against England.

Flight of 31.5.41 (number 111) appears before the flight of 5.5.41 (shown as Number 112) in the Flugbuch.

Schröder showed the overall running total of enemy missions (prior to those on the Russian front) in the Km. column of his Flugbuch.

From Flight 166 Schröder showed his overall running total of enemy missions in the extreme left column of his Flugbuch when they recommenced in Russia, and showed his running tally of Russian missions in the Km. column.

Appendix 4
Flugbuch entries of Fritz Sax

4. Staffel, Zerstörergeschwader 1

Flight No.	Pilot	Crew	Type	Code	Type of Flight	Take-off place	Take-off day	Take-off time	Landing place	Landing day	Landing time	Flight time	Kms.
1472	Sax	Ries	Bf 110	+FP	Transfer flight	Lechfeld	26.5	700	Brün	26.5	710	70	380
1473						Brün		830	Krakau		945	75	400
1474						Krakau		1100	Proskurow		1245	105	600
1475						Proskurow		1320	Uman		1425	65	290
1476						Uman	27.5	1225	Charkow	27.5	1340	75	340
1477						Charkov	29.5	1120	Bjelgorod	29.5	1150	30	120
1478					1. Enemy mission	Bjelgorod	9.6	1010		9.6	1130	80	
1479					2.		10.6	300		10.6	430	90	
1480					3.			530			600		
	Remarks: Shot down: wounded.												
1481	Sax	O'arzt Mohr	Bf 110 F	CJ+SO	Transfer flight	Krakau	28.10.42	1305	Lemberg	28.10.42	1340	35	240
1482						Lemberg	30.10	1330	Uman	30.10	1520	110	420
1483						Uman	31.10	1115	Saporoshje	31.10	1225	75	380
1484						Saporoshje	31.10	1330	Taganrog	31.10	1410	40	270
1485				CF+DP		Taganrog	2.11	1345	Krasnodar	2.11	1445	60	280
1486				+FP		Krasnodar	18.11	1030	Armawir	18.11	1105	35	200
1487						Armawir		1245	Tazinskaja		1350	75	370
1488		Lt. Dreher		+NP		Tazinskaja	24.11	1230	Nowotscherkask	24.11	1330	60	200
1489						Nowotscherkask	25.11	1100	Rostow	25.11	1120	20	35
1490						Rostow	26.11	1210	Krasnodar	26.11	1320	70	280
1491	Sax		Bf 110	S9+BP	Transfer flight	Krasnodar	29.11	1205	Tazinskaja	29.11	1314	69	390
1492		Janke		S9+RN	4. Enemy mission		30.11	545	Krasnodar	30.11	855	130	
1493		Graf			5. Enemy mission		1.12	855	Miljutinskaja	1.12	1020	85	
1494		Lange		+HN	5.	Miljutinskaja	7.12	1129	Tazinskaja	7.12	1150	31	
1495				+HN	6.	Tazinskaja	8.12	610		8.12	725		
1496		Jenig		+RM		Tazinskaja	11.12	1247	Werbowka	11.12	1306		
1497		Hils		+KM	7.	Werbowka	16.12	1345		16.12	1450		
1498		Hils		+SN	8.		17.12	1230		17.12	1335		
1499		Lange		+LN	9.		20.12	11.45		20.12	1240		
1500		Lange		+NN	10.		20.12	1345		20.12	1415		
1501				+FP	Transfer flight		23.12	1230	Salsk	23.12	1315	45	
1502						Salsk	25.12	800	Taganrog Süd	25.12	835	35	
1503						Taganrog Süd	26.12	1310	Rostow West	26.12	1320	10	
1504		Dv. Hoerz	Kl 35	KE+SP	Courier flight	Rostow West	31.12	1140	Schachty	31.12	1250	70	180
1505						Schachty	31.12	1330	Rostow West	31.12	1410	40	120
1506						Rostow	2.1.43	910	Taganrog Süd	2.1.43	930	20	40
1507						Schachty	6.1.43	1015	Rostow	6.1.43	1130	75	
1508						Rostow	7.1.43	1240	Krasnodar	7.1.43	1345	65	180
	Remarks: Emergency landing.												
1509			Bf 110	+SP		Krasnodar	9.1.43	1150	Schachty	9.1.43	1250	60	310
1510	Sax		Bf 110	+SP	Courier flight	Schachty	9.1	1320	Krasnodar	9.1	1425	65	310
1511				SP		Krasnodar	10.1	1330	Schachty	10.1	1435	65	310
1512		Karow		EP	11. Enemy mission	Schachty	12.1	1145		12.1	1217	92	
1513				FN	12.		13.1	1035		13.1	1215	100	
1514				AM	13.		15.1	950		15.1	1042	52	
1515				AM	14.		17.1	835		17.1	930	65	
1516				PM	15.		20.1	845		20.1	940	55	
1517				KH	16.					1355	1440	45	
1518				BM	17.		21.1	1010		21.1	1115	65	
1519				BM	18.					1312	1400	48	
1520				KM	19.		22.1	810		22.1	850	40	
1521				CH	20.					1402	1435	33	
1522				CN	21.		26.1	1000		26.1	1025	25	
1523				HM	22.					1215	1315	60	
1524				HM	23.		27.1	1125		27.1	1230	65	
1525					24.					1345	1440	55	
1526					25.		28.1	1412		28.1	1510	58	
1527					26.		30.1	1000		30.1	1107	67	
1528					27.		31.1	755		31.1	900	65	
1529	Sax		Bf 110	DM	28. Enemy mission	Rostow	2.2	1030	Rostow	2.2	1145	75	
1530				LM	29.					1253	1350	57	
1531				LM	30.		4.2	1410		4.2	1455	45	
1532				HM	31.		5.2	610		5.2	715	65	
1533				SF	32.		6.2	1420		6.2	1500	40	
1534					33.					1510	1545	35	
1535				CH	34.		11.2	622		11.2	745	83	
1536				SM	35.	Kuteinikowo	12.2	615	Kuteinikowo	12.2	725	70	
1537					36.					827	1024	117	
1538				AC	37.		13.2	1302		13.2	1415	49	

Flight No.	Pilot	Crew	Type	Code	Type of Flight	Take-off place	Take-off day	Take-off time	Landing place	Landing day	Landing time	Flight time	Kms.
1539				AM	38.		17.2	1340		17.2	1435	55	
1540					39.		20.2	1000		20.2	1130	90	
1541					40.		21.2	1230		21.2	1305	35	
1542					41.			1415			1500	45	
1543					42.		22.2	1315		22.2	1413	57	
1544					43.			1528			1621	52	
1545				RM	44.		24.2	1020		24.2	1143	83	
1546					45.			1307			1410	63	
1547				FM	46.		25.2	755		25.2	945	110	
1548	Sax	Carow	Bf 110	AC	47.	Dnjepro	25.2	1110	Dnjepro	25.2	1252	102	
1549				CM	48.			1500			1610	70	
1550				AM	49.		26.2	540		26.2	705	105	
1560					50.			930			1055	85	
1561					51.			1330			1520	110	
1562					52.		27.2	548		27.2	725	97	
1563					53.			850			1012	82	
1564				AM	54.		2.3	630		2.3	813	93	
1565					55.			910			1044	94	
1566				SM	56.		4.3	1450		4.3	1640	140	
	Remarks: Emergency landing. Burning.												
1567				AM	57.		13.4	535		13.4	710	95	
1568					58.			910	Poltawa		1055	105	
1569					59.	Poltawa		1330			1525	115	
1570					60.		14.4	1320		14.4	1515	115	
	Remarks: On Bjelgorod!!												
1571				CM	Transfer	München	15.4	1330	Vicenza	15.4	1430	60	380
1572						Vicenza		1510	Iesi		1620	70	400
1573						Iesi	16.4	1020	Foggia	16.4	1130	70	400
1574						Foggia		1400	Gerbini		1530	90	500
1575						Gerbini	18.4	1300	Foggia	18.4	1430	90	500
1576	Sax	Carow	Bf 110	CM	Scramble. Enemy mission	Trapani	18.4	1314		18.4	1430	30	
1577					Shipping escort		19.4	1305	Tunis	19.4	1505	120	
1578					Shipping escort			1635			1735	60	
1579					Transfer	Trapani		1900	Gerbini		1945	45	
1580						Gerbini	21.4	640	Trapani	21.4	729	40	
1581						Trapani		1805	Gerbini		1845	40	
1582				GM	Shipping escort			1045			1145	60	
1583				GM	Enemy mission		26.4	705		26.4	845	40	
1584					Enemy mission			1210			1405	115	
1585					Transporting fuel		27.4	1140		27.4	1225	115	
1586					Transporting fuel			1325			1425	60	
1587					Scramble			1915			2000	45	
1588								1458			1554	56	
1589					Transfer	Gerbini	30.4	715	Trapani	30.4	800	45	
1590					Transporting fuel	Trapani	1.5	900	Tunis	1.5	950	50	
1591						Tunis		1225	Trapani		1320	55	
1592				BC	Scramble	Naples	28.5	1210	Naples	28.5	1340	30	
1593				BC	Shipping escort			803			1130	207	

Notes:
For an unknown reason, flight numbers jump from 1550 straight to 1560.
There is no explanation for flight numbers 1575 and 1576 being for the same time on the same day.

Appendix 5
Flugbuch entries of Edwin Hess

2. Staffel, Zerstörergeschwader 1

These Flugbuch entries are for 1944. Edwin Hess was a Beobachter (Observer) as part of a three-man crew of a Junkers 88 C-6. His name does not appear in his Flugbuch, only those of his pilot and Bordfunker. Edwin Hess showed each enemy mission as a circle in the remarks column of his Flugbuch. Because of the long duration of some of the missions carried out, those which were over 4 hours long counted as 2 sorties, and were shown as 2 circles. Of interest are flights numbers 84 and 85, invasion reconnaissance, which shows that in March 1944 the Germans were already on the look-out for an allied invasion in the Biscay area, far removed from where it eventually took place. As with any clerical record, it is prone to the odd mistake: flight number 86's flight time should read 45 minutes, not 55.

Flight No.	Pilot	Crew	Type	Code	Type of Flight	Take-off place	Take-off day	Take-off time	Landing place	Landing day	Landing time	Flight time	Kms.
79	Uffz. Reichelmann	Gefr. Weisbrod	Ju 88C-6	2N+DH	Transfer flight	Vannes	7.3	1530	Conches	7.3	1640	70	409
80	"	"	"	"	"	Conches	7.3	1705	Evreux	7.3	1716	11	64
81	"	"	"	2N+XK	Bombing practise	Vannes	15.3	0945	Vannes	15.3	1045	60	350
82	"	"	"	"	"	"	"	1118	"	"	1237	79	460
83	"	"	"	2N+FK	Practise flight	"	16.3	0946	"	16.3	1036	50	292
84	"	"	"	+IK	Invasion recon.	"	17.3	1712	"	17.3	2145	273	1530
	Remarks: 1. enemy mission												
85	"	"	"	+BK	"	"	18.3	2002				186	1110
	Remarks: 2. enemy mission												
86	"	"	"	+HK	Practise flight	"	23.3	0937	"	23.3	1022	55	320
87	"	"	"	+HK		"	23.3	1145	"	23.3	1317	92	535
88	"	"	"	+HK	Free Hunt	"	24.3	1024	"	24.3	1516	292	1902
	Remarks: 3. enemy mission												
89	"	"	"	+IK	Emergency sea search	"	25.3	1328	"	25.3	1528	120	700
	Remarks: 4. enemy mission												
90	"	"	"	+FK	Free Hunt	"	31.3	1225	"	31.3	1706	281	1650
	Remarks: 5. enemy mission - 1st enemy contact												
91	Uffz. Reichelmann	Gefr. Weisbrod	Ju 88C-6	+FK	Submarine escort	Vannes	5.4	0732			1132	240	
	Remarks: 6. enemy mission - Crash-landing												
92	Ofw. Thimer	Uffz. Diesler	"	+EK	Transfer flight	Vannes	8.6	1515	Nantes	8.6	1545	30	

The Legion Condor 1936-1939. *Karl Ries & Hans Ring.* This classic book now makes its first appearance in English. This study is one of the few books dedicated to the history of the infamous Legion Condor, the German volunteer unit that fought with pro-Franco forces during the Spanish Civil War from 1936-1939. Many of the tactics and strategies of the Luftwaffe were first formulated and used during operations in Spain. Also, various aircraft were tested and used, such as the famous Ju 87, Do 17, He 111 and Bf 109 - all stalwarts of the later Luftwaffe during World War II. Werner Molders and Adolf Galland first earned their wings as members of the Legion Condor.
Size: 8 1/2" x 11" • 288 pp.
ISBN: 0-88740-339-5 • hard cover • $37.50

The War Diary of Hauptmann Helmut Lipfert: JG 52 On the Russian Front • 1943-1945. *Helmut Lipfert & Werner Girbig.* Aerial combat over the Russian front from one who knew it first hand. Hauptmann Helmut Lipfert's vivid portrayal of his experiences in JG 52 during the last three years of the Second World War will stand as one of the truly classic chronicles of the Jagdwaffe over Russia. This book is a rare view into the air war over Russia, when Luftwaffe pilots accumulated incredible kill tallies while facing overwhelming odds against them in mass assaults.
Size: 6" x 9" • 67 b/w photographs • 224 pp.
ISBN: 0-88740-446-4 • hard cover • $29.95

Jagdeschwader 53: A History of the "Pik As" Geschwader March 1937 - May 1942. *Jochen Prien.* Jagdegeschwader 53 - or as it was better known, the "Pik As" (Ace of Spades) Geschwader - was one of the oldest German fighter units of World War II with its origins going back to the year 1937. This first volume, of a planned three volume set, covers the early years of the Geschwader from its founding in the spring of 1937 up to May of 1942. This book appears here for the first time in English, and contains over 200 additional photos not published in the original German language edition.
Size: 9" x 12" • over 700 b/w and color photographs, aircraft line drawings, maps • 400 pp.
ISBN: 0-7643-0175-6 • hard cover • $89.95

Jagdeschwader 53: A History of the "Pik As" Geschwader Volume 2: May 1942-January 1944 *Jochen Prien.* As with the first volume, this book also appears for the first time in English, and contains over 100 additional photos not published in the original German language edition. The book contains over 450 photographs, revised text and maps, and aircraft line drawings, as well as updated aerial victory and loss listings.
Size: 9" x 12" • over 450 b/w and color photographs, line drawings, maps • 352 pp.
ISBN: 0-7643-0292-2 • hard cover • $89.95

Jagdeschwader 53: A History of the "Pik As" Geschwader Volume 3: January 1944-May 1945. *Jochen Prien.* This third and final part of the narrative starts with the bitter fighting over Italy, where the Geschwaderstab together with I. and III./JG 53 had to face overwhelming odds in their struggle over both the front lines at Cassino and Anzio/Nettuno bridghead, and over northern Italy. This final volume of the epic saga of JG 53 concludes with a list of the officers in command of the Geschwader, its Gruppen and Staffeln, a listing of all known victories claimed by JG 53, strength returns, and other appendices.
Size: 9" x 12" • over 315 b/w photographs, line drawings, profiles, appendices, name index • 464 pp.
ISBN: 0-7643-0556-5 • hardcover • $89.95

JG 54: A Photographic History of the Grunherzjäger. *Held/Trautloft/Bob.* In five turbulent years the members of this highly successful Luftwaffe fighter unit developed into such a close-knit team that even now - almost fifty years later - that bond still exists. This unique photo history was compiled with assistance from the air and ground crews of JG 54. The 400+ photographs document the story of the Grunherz-Geschwader from its formation in the spring of 1939 to the final battles in the courland pocket in the spring of 1945. Within the timespan lay the arduous years of operations in Poland, France, the Channel Front, the Balkans, Russia, Finland and the defense of the Reich.
Size: 7" x 10" • over 400 b/w photographs • 196 pp.
ISBN: 0-88740-690-4 • hard cover • $29.95

Zerstörergruppe: A History of V./(Z)LG 1 - I./NJG 3 • 1939-1941. *Ludwig von Eimannsberger.* This book is the history of V./(Z)LG 1, a Zerstörergruppe (destroyer-group) which, like most of the Luftwaffe destroyer units equipped with the Messerschmitt Bf 110 twin-engined heavy fighter, was disbanded at the end of 1940 after suffering devastating losses during the Battle of Britain. Included are photographs from the personal archives of surviving air—and groundcrewmen—nearly all are previously unpublished. Detailed appendices list casualties, air operations, documents and other data.
Size: 9" x 12" • over 500 b/w photographs • 240 pp.
ISBN: 0-7643-0479-8 • hard cover • $59.95

Six Months to Oblivion: The Defeat of the Luftwaffe Fighter Force Over the Western Front 1944/1945. *Werner Girbig.* This book covers the last chapter, the decline and fall of the air defense of Germany. It is a diary of losses and a chronicle in which the fighter pilot plays the lead. It tells of the young men who joined their squadrons full of optimism and derring-do, only to give their lives to no purpose in a last desperate endeavour. In this unabridged edition, Werner Girbig gives detailed analysis of these last months of the Luftwaffe and the fall of a once mighty air force.
Size: 6" x 9" • 236 pp.
ISBN: 0-88740-348-4 • hard cover • $29.95

Hitler's Fall Guys: An Examination of the Luftwaffe by One of America's Most Famous Aces. *Col. Walker M. "Bud" Mahurin, USAF, (Ret.).* This new book by famed U.S. ace Walker "Bud" Mahurin is an examination of Germany's Luftwaffe by one who fought against them in the skies over Europe, and who befriended them after the war. He considered himself fortunate to get to know leading combat airmen in his own air force, as well as in the United Kingdom and Germany.
Size: 6" x 9" • b/w photographs • 200 pp.
ISBN: 0-7643-0870-X • hard cover • $29.95

The Interrogator: The Story of Hanns Joachim Scharff, Master Interrogator of the Luftwaffe. *Raymond F. Toliver.* This is the story of Hanns Scharff the master interrogator of the Luftwaffe who questioned captured American fighter pilots of the USAAF Eighth and Ninth Air Forces in World War II. This Intelligence Officer gained the reputation as the man who could magically get all the answers he needed from the prisoners of war. In most cases the POWs being interrogated never realized that their words, small talk or otherwise, were important pieces of the mosaic Hanns Scharff was constructing for the benefit of Germany's war effort.
Size: 6" x 9" • over 150 b/w photographs • 352 pp.
ISBN: 0-7643-0261-2 • hard cover • $29.95

JG 7: The World's First Jet Fighter Unit 1944/1945. *Manfred Boehme.* Formed in August 1944, Jagdgeschwader 7 was equipped with the revolutionary Me 262 jet fighter, which was faster than any aircraft in existence at the time. This unit experienced all of the highs and lows associated with the introduction of such a radically new design. Thus the history of JG 7 is also the story of the Me 262, an inspired design which broke new ground in many areas of technology, and for which there was simply not enough time for thorough development. The pilots of JG 7 frequently had to make do with improvisation and faced a numerically far superior enemy in an aircraft which was technically immature. Manfred Boehme has collected many documentary sources including first hand accounts, technical records and photo archives.
Size: 6" x 9" • 168 photographs, line drawings • 288 pp.
ISBN: 0-88740-395-6 • hard cover • $29.95